Inclined to Speak

Inclined to Speak

AN ANTHOLOGY OF
CONTEMPORARY
ARAB AMERICAN POETRY

Edited by Hayan Charara

The University of Arkansas Press
Fayetteville
2008

ISBN-10 (cloth): 1-55728-866-6
ISBN-13 (cloth): 978-1-55728-866-0

ISBN-10 (paper): 1-55728-867-4
ISBN-13 (paper): 978-1-55728-867-7

12   11   10   09   08   6   5   4   3   2

Designed by Liz Lester

⊛ The paper used in this publication meets the minimum requirements of the American
National Standard for Permanence of Paper for Printed Library Materials Z39.48-1984.

LIBRARY OF CONGRESS CATALOGING-IN-PUBLICATION DATA

Inclined to speak : an anthology of contemporary Arab American poetry /
    edited by Hayan Charara.
          p.   cm.
     Includes bibliographical references and index.
     ISBN 978-1-55728-867-7 (pbk. : alk. paper)—ISBN 978-1-55728-866-0
(cloth : alk. paper)
        1. American poetry—Arab American authors. 2. American poetry—
21st century. I. Charara, Hayan, 1972–
     PS591.A7I53 2008
     811′.540808927073—dc22

                                    2007045037

CONTENTS

INTRODUCTION

The history of literature and of criticism demonstrates that if anything is constant in our understanding of the literatures of the world, it is the varied and changing conceptions of those literatures. Identity only further complicates the matter, and for Arab American poetry this also happens to be the sphere toward which most discussions gravitate and the traps from which most Arab American poets work ceaselessly to break free. Whether the thirty-nine poets represented in this anthology like it or not (I would argue that most of them dislike it), identity is, for their readers, typically both an entry and exit point to their poems. It is a troublesome affair—the defining of a people—but it also serves as a starting point for renewal. Without a doubt, the poems here do their part to trouble and reshape any notions of a literature or a people called Arab American.

The term "Arab American" itself is relatively new. Arabs, and Americans of Arab descent, populated the United States, in significant numbers, long before a name for them (one that did not also serve as a slur) became common. Yet the label "Arab American" remains contentious, and this contentiousness illustrates one of the most recognizable products of the polemics of identity: the incredible resistance to any and sometimes all understandings about a collective identity, whether found in literature, politics, or elsewhere, either from within the group or from outside it. Keith Feldman, writing about the historical emergence of the Arab American category, argues that this category "has been implicated historically in the maintenance of exclusionary practices of US racial nationalism, even as it has revealed the contradictions of such practices." For my part, I was also aware of the role that anthologizing Arab American poetry could play in reifying such practices. For better or worse, I relied in great part on the poems collected here to guide any debates (of course, I chose the poems), and again, for better or worse, these poems do what the members of any group generally excel at when it comes to matters of identity: they disagree with each other. They disagree, yes, but in doing so they initiate and foster change, and they resist it too. Each in its own way disrupts the notions and expectations that most people have of Arab Americans, while simultaneously working together, as a body of literature, to express something that is undeniably Arab American, even if this something is always under constant modification. Literally, from poem to poem, and from poet to poet, "Arab American" is accepted, rejected, maintained, and altered.

Homi K. Bhabha puts it this way: identity, as a form of knowledge, operates in such a way that it "allows for the possibility of simultaneously embracing two contradictory beliefs, one official and one secret, one archaic and one progressive, one that allows the myth of origins, the other that articulates difference and division." Bhabha suggests that an identification that simultaneously embraces ambivalence and alterity is impossible to encapsulate in a fixed image. The homogenous object of discourse becomes a heterogeneous subject, one whose "identity" is both true and false, recognized and contested. Walid Bitar fittingly notes in "Survival of the Fittest" that "Our ancestors wouldn't know what to make / of us if they were here." This confusion is not limited to "ancestors" or the past. The individual, in the present moment, must also contend with difference and ambivalence. The poet must negotiate the contradictions between himself and his ancestors, himself and those "unlike" him, as well as between himself and those "almost" like him. While such negotiations can lead to a kind of liberation from identity, they often end up in a tug-of-war between recognizing and rejecting one's subjectivity, as is the case in Lawrence Joseph's "Curriculum Vitae":

> I might have been born in Beirut,
> not Detroit, with my right name.
> Grandpa taught me to love to eat.
> I am not Orthodox, or Sunni,
> Shiite, or Druse. Baptized
> in the one true Church, I too
> was weaned on Saint Augustine.
> Eisenhower never dreamed I wore
> corrective shoes. Ford Motor Co.
> never cared I'd never forgive
> Highland Park, River Rouge, Hamtramck.

In another poem, "Sand Nigger," Joseph highlights both the complexity and the irony of this kind of recognition-rejection of subjectivity. He describes himself as

> an enthusiastically
> bad-tempered sand nigger

who waves his hands, nice enough
to pass, Lebanese enough
to be against his brother,
with his brother against his cousin,
with cousin and brother
against the stranger.

Not surprisingly, tension exists between a totalizing schema of identity (the knowledge, for example, that allows for "the one true Church" to exist) and a "multiplicity of understandings" (Lebanese as "Orthodox," "Sunni," "Shiite," "Druse," "Maronite," not to mention the sort of "American" that would be recognized by Eisenhower and the sort that would not). This is a tension between consensus and disparity, between acceptance and rejection. The problem, however, is that neither space fully accommodates the subject, nor does the space in between. In "Living with Opposition," Elmaz Abinader provides a painful, if not heartbreaking, image of the individual who attempts unsuccessfully to negotiate between these oppositions by trying to suppress the "secret" or "archaic" (in this case the "Arab") in order to become fully accepted by and enmeshed in the "official" (or "American"). She does so in the person of her father, who is dressed in a "very fine" suit, "going to the carnival / at the fireman's hall in his small Pennsylvania / mining town." There, he offers his hand "to all the men in their beer covered tee shirts." No matter how much the father embraces American culture (while keeping back his otherness), his language and appearance betray him and articulate difference and division:

My father
stringing his English together with suits
pressed badly and always
a little too long.

Yet decades of "living with opposition" leave only weariness:

My father strolls around his town
now in the same clothes he wore
twenty years ago. He is not crazy.
He is tired of being foreign, of trying
so hard just to breathe, to get a little light
of his own.

Like so many of the individuals encountered in the poems of this anthology, this father is "stuck" because of an inability, or perhaps even an unwillingness (whether on his part or on the part of the various communities he moves in and out of), to view these types of conflicts and oppositions not as debilitating but rather as points of release from the binds created by competing notions of identity. Instead, he is fighting what appears to be a never-ending battle. He is up against what Edward Said called a "lineage of absolutism," whereby a single, incorporating, and homogenizing historical scheme is developed that will "assimilate non-synchronous developments, histories, cultures, and peoples to it."

Many, however, have found ways of living with opposition, of embracing multiplicity. They have also taken on more than just cultural or national identifications. The idea of a single Arab American poetry (or people, or individual, or culture) is exploded through varied and complicated engagements with language, style, form, meaning, tradition, class, gender, ethnicity, race, nationality, history, ideology, and of course the self. At every turn of the page, the reader finds a poetic interrogation, and the result is almost always a profound discovery, a reformulation, and a new way of seeing the world. A reader searching for a single, totalizing schema will not find it in these poems. However, despite the conflicts and contradictions in the following pages, the poets and poems in this collection argue with each other in a spirit of community, even if this community exists, at times, only in the imagination. For often it does: just as nations, according to Timothy Brennan, "are imaginary constructs that depend for their existence on an apparatus of cultural fictions in which imaginative literature plays a decisive role," so too are the communities that constitute them. However, the atmosphere created by these "imagined communities" (the phrase, of course, is Benedict Anderson's), particularly in the American context, stems in great part from an urgency that arises out of the cultural representation of Arabs and Arab Americans found in academia, journalism, literature, music, art, television, and film. In an issue paper published by the American-Arab Anti-Discrimination Committee, regarding the negative images of Arabs in American popular culture, the author notes that "Americans know a great deal about Arabs. The problem is that so much of what is known is wrong." The task, then, becomes to reverse the scenario. Khaled Mattawa implores Arab American writers to do just this: "If the image of us is truly being created by the American imagination, the time has come to invalidate that image and render it unrecognizable both to ourselves and to the world."

I agree, and this emphasis on rendering the image of "ourselves" unrecognizable served as a driving force behind the decisions I made in selecting the poems for this book. But before I began my own work as an editor, the task had obviously already been at hand for quite some time. For more than half a century, not only have Arab American poets struggled to claim agency for creating the Arab American image, but in doing so they have helped to turn this image on its head. This has been and continues to be a monumental undertaking. Misrepresentations of "Orientals" are so deeply entrenched that Edward Said's powerful critique applies today (to Arabs, as well as to Arab Americans) perhaps even more so than it did when *Orientalism* was published in 1978. Whether in literature, art, television, film, scholarship, or journalism, Arabs and Arab culture are depicted mostly as violent, intolerant, backward, and misogynistic. Indeed, it should not come as a surprise that analysis nearly thirty years old still holds true, for today even highly educated persons draw conclusions about things "Arab" that are nearly indistinguishable from remarks made several hundred years ago. For many—too many—"the Arab" lives in a timeless space where "progress" (as represented by the Arab world's opposite, Western civilization) is at best a hapless dream or even a threat. This is what most Arab Americans discover about themselves when they read Western literature with Arab characters, or watch Americans films set in the Middle East, or study the great European paintings depicting the Orient.

The consequence, sometimes, is for one of these Arabs to set out to claim otherwise. To a degree, all the contributors to this anthology, through poetry, are doing just that. Each poem, in its own way, is an act of invalidating an image that is at best misguided; each contests an uncritical representation, even in the absence of an apparent "political" reference. The moment an "Arab" or "Arab American" distinction is recognized—in the poem, in the poet, in the context of this anthology—it becomes nearly impossible to escape the presumptions that this distinction triggers. In the worst-case scenario, violence and destruction result. Etel Adnan's representation of and response to this can be found in her explosive sequence of poems "The Arab Apocalypse," in which Adnan combines words and images to critique and warn of a worsening political reality for Arabs worldwide, one that, if left uncontested, will spiral toward a modern-day Armageddon. This is a world where "words lose their meaning and become arsenic / . . . roses grow only in cemeteries / . . . the sun itself has no other purpose than being a shroud," where "rats . . . inherit the Heralded Kingdom." In "Almost One," David Williams sounds a similar warning:

> My over-emotional
> nature inclines me to fanatical fantasies. I want to slip
> into terminals and depots, anywhere people wait
> hurriedly, neither here nor there, and seduce them into
> dancing in lines and circles that eventually join hands in
> one great spiral. Otherwise I'm afraid someday they
> might start screaming for blood, if only not to feel so
> small and alone. Such grandiosity and paranoia, not
> uncommon among my kind, is cancelled out by an
> equally characteristic fatalism, which leaves me
> speechless—a condition hard to spot among minorities,
> since we can barely get a word in edgewise.

According to Saladin Ahmed, we are engaged in the "myths of then vs. the myths of now"; he warns, "In a word, brother, it is dangerous." It is dangerous both for those who are constituted in the "myths of now" and for those making these myths. Arab American poets illustrate what Said refers to as "the formidable structure of cultural domination and, specifically for formerly colonized peoples, the dangers and temptations of employing this structure upon themselves or upon others." That is, we may build what we demolish. Yet in this engagement of myth-making and myth-breaking, Arab American poets open doors of possibility—quite revolutionary—that lead to the reinventing of the images of Arab American people, culture, literature, and history. In "Usage," a poem that takes its form from the usage guides found in most dictionaries and English handbooks, Hayan Charara addresses the making and breaking of myths:

> I deceive *myself.* / I will deceive you *myself.* In the Bronx,
> I *passed* as Puerto Rican. I *passed* as Greek in Queens,
> also Brazilian, Pakistani, Bangladeshi, even a famous,
> good-looking American movie actor. As Iranian in Manhattan.

At the mall in New Jersey, the sales clerk guessed Italian.
Where Henry Ford was born, my hometown, I always *pass*
as Arab. / I may look like the men in the great paintings
of the Near East, but their lives, their ways, I assure you,
are in the *past. Plus,* except in those paintings, or at the movies,
I never saw Arabs with multiple wives, or who rode camels,
lived in silk tents, drank from desert wells; *moreover,* it's time
to move past that. . . .

Others in the anthology also echo this notion. Ahimsa Timoteo Bodhrán insists, "We have all been weeds, known the pull of a farmer's hands. // Each of us is indigenous somewhere." When shoppers object to the actions of Mohja Kahf's grandmother, who "puts her feet in the sink / of the bathroom at Sears / to wash them in the ritual washing for prayer," the grandmother instructs the poet to tell them, "My feet are cleaner than their sink. / Worried about their sink, are they? I / should worry about my feet!" Neither the grandmother nor the shoppers are fooled by Kahf's attempts (in Arabic to her grandmother, in English to the shoppers) to feign apologies from either side. However, in a moment of coming together only possible in the world of American consumerism, "we all emerge on the sales floor / and lose ourselves in the great common ground / of housewares on markdown."

In recent years, liberal concepts of identity as expressed in poems like these have come under attack. "Multiculturalism," "hybridity," "political poetry"—all these are, in certain spheres, labels meant to discredit the ideas, literature, or people associated with them. However, the undeniable fact is that more and more, especially in the United States but also around the globe, people tend to identify less with limited social constructions of nationalism and more with those that incorporate what may be called postmodern and/or postcolonial realities. I have argued that the poets here challenge traditional notions, and I cannot stress this point enough. I am certain, too, that the poets here are more than aware of the roles they play in determining cultural constructs. "You read Dante or Shakespeare," Said tells us, "in order to keep up with the best that was thought and known, and also to see yourself, your people, society, and tradition in their best lights. In time, culture comes to be associated, often aggressively, with the nation or the state; this differentiates 'us' from 'them,' almost always with some degree of xenophobia." Said also warns of the "returns" to culture and tradition that such xenophobia often leads to—"rigorous codes of intellectual and moral behavior that are opposed to the permissiveness associated with such relatively liberal philosophies as multiculturalism and hybridity"—and while Arab American culture as expressed in these poems certainly is, in this sense, a source of identity, it is simultaneously a source of difference, of "permissiveness," not only individually (from poet to poet, poem to poem) but especially taken collectively, as a whole. This ultimately makes an anthology of this kind—"ethnic," as it is often called—both worthwhile and an antidote to the dangers of strict notions of identity, whether they are nationalist, ethnic, religious, or otherwise. To this end, the poems here challenge the "returns" that rise either from within the group itself or from outside it.

Another outcome of the challenges to the sustained efforts of others to speak for Arabs and Arab Americans is an upsurge of "native" voices. In 1988, Gregory Orfalea and Sharif S. Elmusa's *Grape Leaves: A Century of Arab American Poetry* collected the work of twenty poets, five of whom, it should be noted, were born in the late 1800s. These "early" poets were the Mahjar, or "emigrant" poets—the most famous of them no doubt Kahlil Gibran. Operating under relatively inclusive criteria for inclusion, Orfalea and Elmusa were able to include in *Grape Leaves* only fifteen Arab American poets not associated with the Mahjar poets. Exactly two decades later, counting only the poets in this anthology (who, it goes without saying, by no means represent *all* Arab American poets), the number of "new" poets has nearly doubled. Of course, without the prerequisite of a "significant publication record," which I imposed on this anthology and will discuss later, it is difficult to say just how many more Arab American poets are writing today. As one Arab American poet whom I "discovered" late in the process told me, "It's not as if we're listed in the Yellow Pages."

Plenty of indicators, however, suggest a large group. The Radius of Arab American Writers (RAWI), a literary organization, boasts a membership of close to three hundred writers, scholars, and artists, many of them poets. Another such marker is the publication, in recent years, of several anthologies centered in some respect around the larger and more established body of writings by Arab Americans, including *Post Gibran: Anthology of New Arab American Writing,* edited by Munir Akash and Khaled Mattawa; *Food for Our Grandmothers: Writings by Arab-American and Arab-Canadian Feminists,* edited by Joanna Kadi; *The Poetry of Arab Women,* edited by Nathalie Handal; Susan Muaddi Darraj's *Scheherazade's Legacy: Arab and*

Arab American Women on Writing; and *Dinarzad's Children: An Anthology of Contemporary Arab American Fiction,* edited by Pauline Kaldas and Khaled Mattawa. In a special issue on Arab American literature, the journal *MELUS* (*Multi-Ethnic Literature in the United States*) noted the growing academic interest in this group and its literature, citing the "impulse to include writing by Arab Americans in US ethnic literature courses, incorporate panels on Arab American culture into national conferences, and to publish edited volumes on the histories of Arab Americans."

None of this is shocking, certainly not to Arab American writers or to those who have followed or studied Arab American literature. Yet to most audiences, the presence of so many Arab American writers is typically a source of astonishment. A void exists, yes, but it has very little to do with a lack of writers or writings. RAWI's membership alone attests to this. Yet most anthologies of American literature, fiction or poetry, old or new, unless they deal thematically with Arab Americans, directly (like this one) or indirectly, rarely include an Arab American writer, much less a number of them—this despite the fact that since September 11, 2001, interest in Arabs and Arab culture is probably greater than ever before in American history. Salah D. Hassan and Marcy Jane Knopf-Newman point this out in their introduction to the *MELUS* special issue: "Despite the increased interest resulting from US domestic and foreign policies, Arab American cultural production continues to sit largely beyond the scope of cultural criticism." Affiliations with Arab or Arab American identity aside, most of the poets in this book have built reputations without much reliance on their Arab American backgrounds. Nor have their accomplishments necessarily been a result of anything Arab American. Many of the poets in this anthology have had their poems appear in some of the nation's and the world's most respected literary publications. Also found here are winners of and finalists for the National Book Award, the American Book Award, the Yale Younger Poets prize, and the Pushcart Prize, as well as recipients of fellowships from the National Endowment for the Arts, the National Endowment for the Humanities, the Guggenheim Memorial Foundation, and the Lannan Foundation. Many have earned international reputations, their writings translated into dozens of languages. One was the first poet laureate of the Commonwealth of Pennsylvania. Yet except for a small number, the poets gathered here remain mostly unknown not only to the larger public but even to "experts" in the field of contemporary American poetics and to other poets.

The irony, which is almost never lost on a reader who delves deeply into contemporary Arab American poetry, is how unapologetically American the poems can be. This is evident on a literal level. More than English, an "American" language and American sensibilities dominate. How else to figure when Matthew Shenoda writes, "Ain't no three strikes in the world I live in," or when Lawrence Joseph remarks, "I answer, 'What you care?' to a woman who shouts, 'What you want?'" The sense of place in these poems, too, is predominantly American. That is to say, the urge found in many "early" poems by Arabs writing in English to return to the past (to an Arab past, geographically and imaginatively located in the Arab world) is not as strong in the contemporary context; in many ways, it is all but absent. There are "returns" (take, for example, those poems that deal with the reality of an American presence in the Arab world via politics, military presence, commerce, and so on), but the Arab world in these poems is not an idyllic, longed-for, picture-perfect place from way back when. To the contrary, reading a poem written by an Arab American, a reader often finds a much more realistic (if not larger) image of the Arab world than she would on television or in the newspapers.

Otherwise, the places in these poems are unmistakably American. Adele Ne Jame's poems are themselves "fieldwork" done from the Midwest to California to her home in Hawaii. Or consider the home belonging to Pauline Kaldas's aunt, from which one can see "the house of the man who owns *Kentucky Fried Chicken*"; or the town in Jack Marshall's "Appalachia Suite," where the "churchbells chime / 'Summertime, and the livin' is easy.'" Even when a poem is situated outside the United States, the sense of an American space *inside* the poem dominates, as is the case in Khaled Mattawa's "Growing Up with a Sears Catalog in Benghazi, Libya," where the idea of an "imagined community" is invoked in the most unexpected way when a young Mattawa imagines himself camping with a Sears underwear model

> in the $42 Coleman tent,
> the two of us fishing
> at a lake without mosquitoes,
> sailing the boat on page 613.

D. H. Melhem's epical sequence *Country: An Organic Poem,* which literally traverses the entire American landscape, coast to coast, is reminiscent of Walt Whitman in its breath and vision.

Yet for a good number of the poets represented here, no single space appropriately defines where they locate themselves or their poems. Etel Adnan, for instance, writes in both English and French and divides her time between Paris and the Bay Area, and her poems spend as much time *in* the Middle East as they do in Europe or the United States. Eliot Khalil Wilson's poems inhabit the most American of spaces, those nearby (a coal mine, a Salvation Army, a tattoo parlor) and those, too, far away (the Song Ngan Valley in Vietnam, the orchard an immigrant left behind to come to America). The sense of place in Naomi Shihab Nye's poems is undoubtedly international in scope, and she reflects this in her work not only as a poet but also as an editor, a children's book author, and a fiction writer, boundaries crossing each other and at times disappearing altogether. Such "multiplicity" is quite common among the poets in this book. Nathalie Handal (poet, playwright, editor) was born in Haiti and has lived and worked in Europe, the Caribbean, Latin America, the Arab world, and the United States; the international tone of her poems, as well as their witnessing of (often tragic) experiences in all of these places, reflects the hybridity of identity so common among Arab Americans. So too does the poetry of Walid Bitar, who was born in Beirut; emigrated to Canada; and has since worked and traveled in the Middle East, Europe, Asia, and of course the United States. Zaid Shlah, who was born in Canada, lives in the United States, and is of Iraqi descent, cannot help but locate his long sequence "Thirty-Three Beads on a String" in Iraq, not only because of his connection to an Iraqi past but also, and perhaps even more so, because of his ties to an American present. Arguably, every poet in this collection makes use of American history, culture, sociopolitics, or vernacular, so much so that it is often taken for granted that their writings are American or Anglophone.

Technically speaking, none of the poets in this collection are actually permanent residents of an Arab country, and many were not born in the Arab world. However, regardless of distances of time, space, language, or nationality, complete detachment from the Arab world seems to be all but impossible for Arab American poets. They return to this community again and again. Saladin Ahmed addresses the imaginary lines that connect the Arabs of old to the Arabs of today when he thinks of the medieval Arab philosopher Ibn Sina hard at work. Ahmed asks: "How can he be so calm, hearing the bombs fall / on his family, only a thousand years away?" Sam Hamod eulogizes not only the passing of his ancestors but also "the wrong names" they were buried with: "Na'aim Jazeeney, from the beautiful valley / of Jezzine, / died as Nephew Sam." Jack Marshall knows that such imaginary lines can be simultaneously real and imagined. He makes this clear in "Place in the Real," noting too that the "line" between ancestry and self (between past and present) does not have to traverse centuries to seem lost; he needs only to look as far back as his father's relatives: "Except for an obscure / oddball uncle or two, we hardly knew / his side."

Given the American relationship to the Arab world, strained as it is, involvement with it is all but inevitable. In fact, engagement with the political, especially in terms of U.S. policy in the Middle East, seems to bring Arab Americans together more than any other experience. Hosam Aboul-Ela argues that "if anything unites them and separates them from the larger communities in which they live, it is a common acute feeling toward US foreign policy in the Middle East, an engagement with and an attention toward America's role in the region that is not shared by the citizenry as a whole, which might feel engaged at moments of crisis but is easily distracted by domestic culture and politics." The linking of Arab American identity and U.S. foreign policy—an unofficial association, in part, between Arabs and terrorism and threats to national security—is echoed by Salah D. Hassan, who "dates the 'contemporary racialization of Arabs' back to the '60s." The political found in so many of the poems written by Arab Americans can easily be read as a response to these associations, and the link to the Middle East, via U.S. foreign policy, is almost always present.

Palestinians, Iraqis, Lebanese, Saudis, Egyptians, and other Arabs constitute a significant portion of the fabric that is American politics. The poets here certainly "visit" these people and their affairs, and in many cases, the experiences of these Arabs are their own. Sinan Antoon traveled back to his native Baghdad to codirect a documentary about Iraqis in post-Saddam Iraq, yet often when he addresses the Iraq war, and the Iraqi people (even the dead, as in "A Letter"), he does so from abroad—from New York. The question then—perhaps unfair but often asked—is whether he does so as an Iraqi or an American. A recent article in the *New York Times* featuring Arab American authors suggested that Arab Americans "have a sense of doubleness" and are torn between "tradition" on the one hand and "their new culture" on the other. While somewhat of a simplification—not to mention a bit condescending to the majority of Arab Americans, who would hardly consider American culture to be "new" or to have been given to them—the idea of "doubleness" does rightly suggest a very complicated reality for Arab Americans. To borrow again from Bhabha, the space occupied by many Arab Americans is a "Third Space," one that is here and there, as well as neither here nor there. Understandably, many of these writers find themselves addressing the question of belonging. Marian Haddad phrases it succinctly: "I have no history here." In her poem by the same title, it is apparent that "here" can easily be the Middle East or the United States. Either place presents a conundrum (one that is quite common) in terms of situating a history.

Also relevant to a growing number of Arab Americans is the absence of a "personal" history of the Middle East. It simply does not exist for many of them, especially for those whose families were among the first waves of Arabs to immigrate to the United States. Such a personal history tends to belong more to a father or mother, or to grandparents, or to even more distant relatives. But the connection remains strong; it is *kept* strong. When Kevin Gerard Rashid writes, "My father's people say / never to give or accept / knives as gifts," he keeps to that belief. He personalizes his history, and his father's people become his own. The same can be said, in terms of such historical personalization, of Gregory Orfalea. That a bomb has fallen on his "great-uncle's newly- / irrigated fields" carries no less personal significance because the field is several thousand miles away from Orfalea's home in California.

For some, an American history—personal and public—is being newly created and comes *after* one that began elsewhere. Diaspora is a recurring theme among many new Arab American poets. Khaled Mattawa, for instance, came to the United States from Libya. Suheir Hammad was born in a Palestinian refugee camp. Others have taken the opposite route, so to speak, and have left the United States: Lisa Suhair Majaj, for example, moved from Massachusetts to the island of Cyprus; Sharif S. Elmusa, once a resident of Washington, D.C., now teaches in Cairo.

Wherever they are, however much they address things Arab or Arab American, in the contemporary context, one of the most significant events for Arab Americans occurred on September 11, 2001, when hijackers took over four airplanes and crashed two into the World Trade Center towers in New York City, one into the Pentagon, and one in a field in Pennsylvania. Arguably no other happening served more to reify Arab American identity. The 1995 bombing of the Alfred P. Murrah Federal Building in Oklahoma City had earlier brought to light the immediate associations made between

terrorism and Arabs (specifically Muslim Arabs, though often this distinc-
tion is not made). While these sorts of assumptions predated the Oklahoma
City bombing, the contemporary "problem" of such generalizations became
evident when it was realized that "homegrown" terrorists Timothy McVeigh
and Terry Nichols—not Arabs—had carried out the attack. None of this
seemed to matter much a little over six years later, after the world discov-
ered, bit by horrifying bit, that nineteen Arab men were responsible for the
worst attack of terrorism ever enacted against the United States. If ever
"Arab" was synonymous with "terrorist," it was on this most infamous of
dates. Suheir Hammad's poem "First Writing Since" articulates a fear many
Arab Americans felt that Tuesday afternoon:

> first, please god, let it be a mistake, the pilot's heart failed,
> the plane's engine died.
> then please god, let it be a nightmare, wake me now.
> please god, after the second plane, please, don't let it be anyone
> who looks like my brothers.

D. H. Melhem adds yet another common sentiment expressed by Arab
Americans in the aftermath of 9/11: "Staunch my terrible wounds / and heal
your own thereby."
   Regrettably, many Americans still register the complaint that since the
attacks, Arabs, Muslims, Arab Americans, and Muslim Americans have not
spoken out enough against violence and terrorism. Most regrettable is the
fact that this presumption is simply false. They have spoken out, and they
have done so regularly, loudly, and in great numbers. Not a single Arab
American poet in this anthology has overlooked the question of violence—
how could any American poet, Arab or otherwise, reasonably do so? Tending
to get overlooked are rational and responsible Arab American voices, espe-
cially those offering compassion and those offering complex perspectives.
Yes, they are provided space to "speak." Generally, though, preference (time,
space, and attention) is given to more sinister Arabs, the likes of Osama bin
Laden, or Abu Musab al-Zarqawi; or to Arab "experts," who espouse ide-
ologies so extreme or far-flung, or so politically motivated, that they can-
not be taken seriously, at least not as representative of Arab American
interests. As a matter of necessity, then, Arab Americans (and many poets
are among those at the forefront) work rigorously to dismantle the mis-

guided and imbalanced (if not wholly irresponsible) images and knowledge otherwise produced. It is out of this atmosphere, which goes nearly unquestioned by a large majority of the public (professional or otherwise), that David Williams writes: "So many people can't wait to tell us, with a mathematician's pride, that they've got us figured out. Most generalizations, mine included, are blunt instruments." From this, too, stems the frustration expressed by Elmaz Abinader: "Someone has told you, It's an attitude problem. / I hear this, say something like, I wonder whose."

I have wondered, too, especially after several years of deliberately and intensely reading Arab American poetry, what aspect of being Arab American is most misunderstood. While deconstructing stereotypes and political violence (particularly against the Palestinians, and more recently in Iraq and Lebanon) take prominence in the poems of Arab Americans, another matter tends to prevail in public and mainstream discourses. Ironically, it is also perhaps the most easily remedied misconception people have of Arabs and Arab culture: the conflation of "Arab" with "Islam." For most Arabs, the use of these two disparate terms interchangeably across large portions of American and European societies only further reinforces how little the "West" attempts to understand the cultures of the Middle East and of Islam. On the one hand, this error seems outlandish, almost laughable—one needs only to look up the words in a dictionary or do the most cursory research to discover why "Arab" does not necessarily equal "Islam"; or note that a large number of Arab Americans are Christian (a majority, depending on the source); or recognize the fact—quite puzzling to some—that there are among Arabs (not just Arab Americans) those with a Jewish heritage.

Perhaps one of the most overlooked aspects of Arab American culture is the existence of queer Arabs and queer writing. In many cultures, pervasive fear and hostility toward people who are gay, lesbian, transsexual, or transgender dominate. When asked to explain the execution of gay men in his country, President Mahmoud Ahmadinejad told an audience in New York City, "In Iran we don't have homosexuals like in your country." The crowd responded with jeers and laughter, but even in the United States gays and lesbians daily experience violence, and they are among the few groups for whom discrimination is being written back into law—prohibitions on gay marriage, for instance. And while Arab American poets—some of whom are "out"— have not disregarded the matter (they have challenged and complicated taboos and stereotypes, and they have celebrated and recognized queer life), this subject goes mostly unremarked. In anthologies and studies devoted to Arab American literature, it receives little attention. There are obviously exceptions. In her introduction to *Food for Our Grandmothers,* Joanna Kadi announces that we are "lesbians, bisexuals, and heterosexuals," but at the same time she also notes, "many of our experiences and histories are still to be explored." Though this anthology gives the matter brief attention, I hope it encourages more engagement.

The poets exploring these and other issues invite us to examine them further, if not for the first time, and often their poems speak to us in the hope that a more honest and accurate understanding will be reached. But "truth" alone will not solve these problems, not entirely. Said insists that we "ought never to assume that [this] . . . structure of lies or of myths . . . , were the truth about them to be told, would simply blow away." What needs to be done is to dismantle the discourses (note the plural) that create and maintain this structure. To this end, as I have mentioned before, the poets represented here are actively involved in and acutely aware of the task at hand. Matthew Shenoda recognizes the power of language in this regard: "Incessant, pushing for the struggle / of re-generation." He also understands "that nothing happens without a declaration / even independence," and so, "We break things down to the critical / so that each generation can link to the next / without severance." Sam Hazo speaks directly to the role of the poet, and of the poem, when it comes to defiance: "I choose to mount / my mutiny in words"; by doing so, Hazo makes his "creed defiance."

Obviously, not every poet in this anthology implicitly deals with "political" issues or with matters that, on the surface, lend themselves easily to such discussions, theoretical or otherwise; of course, neither do all the poems I have chosen. It goes without saying that the poets here who have engaged the political, the social, and the cultural, in Arab American terms, do not necessarily do so all the time. Nor is political engagement by any means mandatory or even remotely essential for inclusion in this anthology or what we are now calling Arab American poetry. Suheir Hammad, Nathalie Handal, Lisa Suhair Majaj, and Naomi Shihab Nye, among others, are often recognized as spokespersons for the struggle of the Palestinian people. However, each of them also "speaks" to a multitude of other "issues" (particularly but not only as women of color), as well as to other cultures and people—that is, not only to Arabs. When the poet June Jordan announced, "I was born a Black woman / and now / I am become a Palestinian," she expressed solidarity with more than a people. Solidarity of this sort transcends official categories, and it is never a one-way relationship. Even when a poet does not deal directly with issues that are generally associated with Arab Americans, it would be irresponsible to assume that the content, and the form, do not speak to the Arab American experience. Alise Alousi's meditation on "lipstick," and Kazim Ali's on cultural icons, music, and art, are as much a part of an Arab American experience as is the rolling of grape leaves ("Making Meshi"), portrayed by Philip   Metres.

This is something that the reader and the critic must not forget. Rarely is the integrity of the "American" in Arab American (or any other "ethnic" American literature) questioned, especially not over what the poet does or does not write about. But too often, the poet's "Arabness" is questioned, usually because of what he or she does *not* write about. The integrity of the poet's identity (on either side of the hyphen) must be vehemently defended. To treat the poets here any differently would be a dangerous step in the wrong direction.

Still, while it may be, as Edward Said claims, "very easy to argue that knowledge about Shakespeare or Wordsworth is not political," quite the opposite is true when it comes to knowledge about Arabs or Arab Americans. Whether we like it or not, we are political—and not just as Arabs. Nuar Alsadir, Hedy Habra, Lara Hamza, Sekeena Shaben, and Deema K. Shehabi are, for instance, among the many "new" Arab American poets who challenge notions about women in American, Arab, and Arab American culture. They do so by confronting form, content, and yes, even identity. But identity is not the sole or even the most important aspect of their work. Yet emerging Arab American poets have entered the public sphere at a moment when the very notions of "Arab" and "Arab American" are ready to burst. We are ripe for reinvention. Fady Joudah, a physician and one of the poets in the collection, puts it perfectly: "Between what should and what should not be / Everything is liable to explode." In this regard, I am fully aware that this anthology remains deficient.

We are also ripe for criticism. Steven Salaita insists that Arab American literature is becoming "a serious force within the broad category of American letters," and as such he urges and anticipates the growth of Arab American literary criticism. While an immediate concern may be "the external interpretation, acceptance and humanization of Arab Americans and the Arab people as a whole," the emergence of Arab American literature provides critics with exciting areas of scholarship that have been otherwise little explored. Earlier, I briefly mentioned queer studies as an important field of critical inquiry; related to it, of course, is the larger area of feminism. In addition to applying feminist critiques to Arab American literary works, it is important to also note the influence feminist criticism has had on Arab Americans and their writings. These and many other concerns deserve careful surveys, and obviously they must extend far beyond the limits of this introduction.

Encountering several decades of Arab American poetry at once—as I have over the past several years, and as readers will in this anthology—it is difficult not to wonder, through the striking parallels among even the most different poetic sensibilities, if Arab American poets have not created their own aesthetic, or their own criteria for the Arab American narrative, which has for quite a long time now been told by someone else. The answer, I would argue, is yes. This has been accomplished, in part, by their taking-on the notion of hybridity—both expressing and embodying it. In this context, too, Arab American poets have made a clear decision: to choose complexity over any sort of "positive" or "apologetic" image of Arab American culture. Despite the pervasive stereotyping and Orientalizing of Arab and Arab American culture, the poets here have refused to participate in anything less than a challenge to those stereotypes and discourses, regardless of where they come from. This, too, is perhaps where an Arab American literary form originates. It is precisely how these poets approach the subjects and themes of their poems, and not necessarily the themes or subjects themselves, that distinguishes them. There are no "good Arabs" (meaning those who "know their place") behind any of these poems, or any typical poets either—none of them accommodate tradition (ethnic, cultural, or literary) without examining first the cost of such an accommodation. Even if accommodations are made, they are often subverted. These poets have accepted, and their poems have postulated, that the prevailing condition of Arab Americans is complicated, complex, and impossible to pin down in a single poem, or a single image, or even a single anthology. The prevailing condition is also a starting point from which Arab American literature, and identity, can be liberated from any encompassing narratives. Positive or negative images matter little in this regard. Rather, challenges to the "acceptable" narratives provided for Arab Americans matter most.

I have spent such a great deal of time on matters of identity and culture, and the "challenges" faced and made by Arab American poets, I worry that the reader may miss a major thread running through the poems collected here: these poems celebrate life. They do so even in the face of mounting obstacles, and they do so with beautiful, dazzling language. However pleasant or unpleasant the reality (whether it is placed in the poem or not), the poets here embrace it, make it their own, and without hesitation give it up to the world to share. If contemporary Arab American poetry is to be judged political, it is so mostly in this regard.

I feel that I should also note what should, after reading the poems here, be obvious: not only have Arab American poets provided ways for rethinking notions of identity, but they have done the same in terms of poetics—that is, they "experiment" and as such have contributed to reconsiderations of such literary concerns as language, form, metaphor, syntax, and so on. I expect, and hope, that Arab American poetry will more often become the subject of critiques dealing with these "literary" concerns, from which, in large part, they have been excluded.

Early on, and with a straight face, I made a decision not to draw conclusions about Arab Americans. I believed I could choose poems based on artistic quality, place them beside each other, and in doing so be immune from formulating claims about Arab Americans or Arab American poetry. Even the ordering of the poets—alphabetical—I presumed would not allow for this or that pronouncement. Now I realize how impossible the act of "not-concluding" actually is. I was thinking much like the anthropologist who believes he can enter a culture without leaving something of himself in it, or without taking something from it. In other words, believing one can remain neutral is pure fantasy. The undeniable fact is that I cannot claim immunity from making conclusions about Arab American culture, or poetry, or identity. The ways in which I have done so are innumerable, and I have tried to explain myself as clearly as possible with regard to these critical formulations and to be as responsible as possible with them. In this respect, I would like to discuss briefly the process of compiling this anthology and some of the choices that determined its shape and content.

In choosing the poets and poems included in *Inclined to Speak,* I acted deliberately and carefully. Always, my allegiance was to the overall power of the poem rather than to its author or its subject. At the onset, I accepted the possibility that not a single poem necessarily had to deal directly with anything obviously "Arab" or "Arab American." To be honest, I do not know precisely what these two terms entirely represent, and this, I insist, is a good thing. Also, the matter of ethnicity posed a serious dilemma. I did not want to enter into a debate, either with others or with myself, about who is or is not an Arab American. It is not a simple matter. In fact, among "Arab Americans" or "Americans of Arab descent," the issue of who belongs and how to define the group is, as they say, a bag of worms. As for a poet's identification with Arab American identity or Arab American literature, I relied mostly on the individual's acceptance or disavowal of this broad, problematic category. Haas H. Mroue, for instance, does not identify as an Arab American, but rather as an Arab poet who happens to write in English; he does, however, view much of his poetry as Arab American. Needless to say, no poet was excluded from the anthology because of issues of membership in the Arab American community, literary or otherwise.

The only prerequisites for consideration were that the poems be written in English and that the poets have a "substantial publication record." The latter imposed the most limitations. Because of this, many fine young poets were not invited, or they were regretfully declined inclusion. Of course, despite its intentional vagueness, I could have simply done away with the publication requirement. However, I felt it necessary. While it is the case that Arab American writers have typically found it difficult to publish in mainstream presses (despite an overwhelming demand for writings from Arabs and Arab Americans), the arena of poetry has been, perhaps, the most open to Arab Americans, often because of the efforts of small, independent publishers, who have for a long time kept poetry, regardless of group, alive and well. That said, I also wished to create a singular space where the major work of Arab Americans could be found. While for some this collection will feel familiar, for most it will serve as a starting point from which an exploration of the larger bodies of work sampled here may begin. In order to allow for this to be the case, I had to impose a degree of exclusivity. More than anything, my hope is that readers will move from "here" (the anthology) to "there" (the individual books of Arab American poets, the journals that feature Arab American poetry, the anthologies that will follow this one). An anecdote about Elizabeth Bishop tells us that she practiced pinning incomplete poems on a notice board, with gaps that were eventually filled in with the "right" words—sometimes this took weeks, sometimes months. Bishop's refusal to rush a poem to its finish was her way of saying "that the poem's special life had to be honored above her own need for closure or publication." Like Bishop's incomplete poems, this project, I believe, will always remain unfinished. I claim without hesitation and with absolute certainty that this anthology does not represent in any way, shape, or form a definitive collection of Arab American poetry. As I have suggested throughout, this is an ongoing endeavor, and Arab American poetry is a constantly emerging literature, one still in its early stages. Sooner rather than later, the task of revising this anthology, if not completely rethinking it, will be required; any poets not included here for lack of publication, or for any other reason, may later find their poems filling the gaps created by omissions or oversights on my part.

Of American poetry in the twentieth century, J. D. McClatchy says that it is up to us, the readers, to listen and to judge. "Listen sympathetically," he writes, but "judge sternly. What's finally at stake is *you,* your sense of the world, what intimations you have of your own soul, illuminated and shadowed by the poets gathered here." In this spirit, I ask that here at the start of the twenty-first century, reading Arab American poetry, we do the same. These poems are speaking to you, the reader; they are in conversation with you; and they need you to hear them, and to participate with them, now more than ever. I have little doubt that if you listen, you will find here yourself, your sense of the world, and the intimations you have of your own soul.

Hayan Charara

Inclined to Speak

AN ANTHOLOGY OF
CONTEMPORARY
ARAB AMERICAN POETRY

Elmaz Abinader

Elmaz Abinader is the author of *Children of the Roomje*, the first memoir about Arab Americans published in the United States by a trade press. A second memoir, *From This Country*, chronicles her Arab upbringing in a small Appalachian town. Abinader's book of poetry, *In the Country of My Dreams . . .*, which has been described as "expansive" and possessing an "enduring tenderness," won the Josephine Miles/Pen Oakland Award. She has read her poems and, along with the Country of Origin Band, presented her plays to audiences throughout the Middle East, Central America, Europe, and the United States. She lives in Oakland and teaches at Mills College.

Living with Opposition

1. Big Differences

Someone has told you, It's an attitude problem.
I hear this, say something like, I wonder whose,
and drop my head backward into the bath.
You walk still standing at the door.
I feel my hair pull away, surrounding my head
like a spiked crown.
I cannot hear you.

It's an attitude problem, like my father,
you observed, going to the carnival
at the fireman's hall in his small Pennsylvania
mining town. He wore a blue suit,
very fine, Italian maybe or even
Brazilian. He offered his hand
to all the men in their beer covered tee shirts
Jimmy, how you doing?
You pointed this out to me. My father

stringing his English together with suits
pressed badly and always
a little too long. I turned my foot
around in the gravel, began to dig
an escape tunnel.

Your head blocks the light from the hall.
You watch my face float on the water—
a gory lily pad. What I want to say
is you had your chance: your small town,
its pleasant white cross on the Lutheran
church; everyone deep in thought about the chemical
destruction of crab grass.
You lost your concentration
on little things.

I rise from the water and do not turn to look
at my face going under. It's looking
at me walk to you and touch you.

2. Breathing Room

The trees crashed their tops together and I wondered
what the sound was like: the unearthing of the forest?
The wooden clappers vibrating in my church ears? We kissed
the feet of Jesus on the cross that Good Friday. No bells,
only wood beating the walls, the stained glass, the hands
held tightly, the eyes wandering away.

The cedars beneath the cottonwoods cannot hurl themselves
against the long white trunks. What sun they get
filters through the swaying of the top branches
beneath the booming of the larger trees who would pay
to see them swallowed in darkness.

The first city apartment we had shuddered
under the vibrations of jets in and out
of LaGuardia. They turned the t.v.
into a fun mirror, blurring the faces, throwing
the bodies into uncontrolled gyrations.
You slumped onto an elbow, held up your head
and wondered if all of life were like that—
ducking and shaking when things flew overhead.
The moon was fake, you said; only a pizza pan.

3. A Habit of Mind

I know you are not surprised, but I am asked,
why we live apart now. Because we can
is what I tell them. I do not say
that the river running by your house
is bordered by scallops of thick snow,
that the fence posts are staffs
and the wires, lines waiting for notes to perch
like magpies, and when I visit,
I take your hand and ski
confidently through the forest and never fall
and am never noticed.

As I hold each log, one after the other,
they crumble on me. Pricks of bark
and blond dust cover my clothes.
I feed the fire in your woodstove
and watch the air catch the flame
and pull it up through the vent
out to the sky. We hear its breathing
in the next room afraid to get out of bed
until the house is warm, until we can stand,
your long arms wrapping my bare shoulders

watching the snow cradle in the branches
of the trees on your mountainside.

4. The Master Plan

In the city I walk alone blindly
clutch my bags against my body;
check my pockets for change to give
to the ones who call me familiarly
and in need. It does not bother me,
because at the other end of this life
you are sitting beside a blue lamp,
your body quite still, your outline
unwavering. The fire burns slow
and steady. I prefer you there:
blind to a glow that may be a lamp post
or a star.

My father strolls around his town
now in the same clothes he wore
twenty years ago. He is not crazy.
He is tired of being foreign, of trying
so hard just to breathe, to get a little light
of his own.

You thought the moon in New York
deceived you. I go out and look
at the same sky and wait
for the flashing lights of jets.
I ignore the rumble of the subway
nearby. It does not shake me
or brush the trees. I watch
for your flight. My smooth

unsplintered hands rub away
the cold. I watch for that single
meteor; the one that plunges you here
and away again.

What We Leave Behind

Winter pushes into my room. I waken
    And walk to the porch. Windows rattle
Threats of falling. Fragments of glass,
    Veins of dark wood.
I hold the window sill, watch the trees
    Struggle in the cold. Winter mists
From my mouth. Invisible fire.

Cold flattens against our cheeks, faces us
    Steals the warmth from the goblets
Cupped in our hands. The sun cannot
    Sink into tops of our shoulders.
We do not walk the field from end to end.
    A name you hear makes you shiver;
The pages I am writing mark my day.

When I place my hand upon the glass,
    The print released is no longer mine.
I do not want to be alone. Without amber.
    Without the steam rising on a city street.
Back in my room is a whirlpool of light
    I leave thumbprint and palm, and the porch
Becomes ruins behind me.

This House, My Bones

Enter the house,
Sit at the table covered in gold
A cloth, Sitt embroidered
For the third child's birth.
Take the tea, strong and minty,
Hold the glass warm
Against your palms, fragrances
Of centuries fill you, sweetness
Rises up to meet you. The youngest boy
Fuad, shows you a drawing
He has made of a horse
You touch his shoulder, stroke
His hair, he loves to talk to strangers
Show them his room filled with posters
Of extinct and mythical animals: dinosaurs,
Unicorns, dragons. You want to linger
In the music of his voice, afraid his disappearance
Is inscribed on shell cases stockpiling in the Gulf.

Enter the mosque,
Admire the arches
Inlaid with sea colored pebbles,
Follow the carpets, long runners
Of miracles in thread, your feet still damp
Slip against the marble floor.
Spines of men curl into seashells
In the room ahead. Echoes
Of the muezzin shoot around you
Fireworks of speeches and prayers.
Don't be afraid because they worship
Unlike you. Be afraid that worship

Becomes the fight, faith the enemy;
And yours the only one left standing.

Some one asks, what should we do
While we wait for the bombs, promised
And prepared? How can we ready ourselves?
Do we gather our jewelry and books,
And bury them in the ground? Do we dig
Escape tunnels in case our village is invaded?
Do we send our children across the border
To live in refugee camps remembering us
Only in dreams, ghostly voices calling their names?
What do we pack? The coffee urn father
Brought from Turkey? The pair of earrings
Specially chosen for the wedding day?
How can we ever pack anything if not everything?
If not the tick on the wall marking
The children's growth, if not the groan
Of the washing machine in the kitchen,
If not the bare spot on the rug
Where Jidd put his feet when he read
The Friday paper?
Help them gather things: brass doorknobs,
Enamel trays, blue glasses made in Egypt,
Journals of poetry, scraps of newspapers, recipes
They meant to try. And what about the things
They cannot hold? The beginning of life and all
The memories that follow. The end of life
And all that is left to do.

Enter the heart
Read the walls and all the inscriptions
The love of lovers, of children and spouses,

The love of stars, and cardamom and long eye lashes.
Tour the compartments telling
The story: that life was begun with faith,
That life may end with folly. See it heave
In fear that threats, predictions and actions
Are a history already written, spiraling,
Loose and out of control. No amount of hope
Can save it. No amount of words can stop it.
Hold the heart. Imagine it is yours.

The Birds

Minnesota

We stand ankle deep in the lake
    and watch four pelicans:
        air force jets in formation
        arch smokeless in the sky.
I remember them from old cartoons with fish
    hanging from one side of their mouths.
You wrap a towel around your shoulders
    and return to the tent.
        I swim toward the horizon
        piercing the water
        with their shadows.

Nebraska

We creep along gravel roads.
Words drop like tiny metal balls.
    You stop for silence.
        A hawk rises

in front of us,
The only light falls
on his wings, expanding
                        expanding
then it shines onto the rabbit hanging
            limply from his talons.
We see nothing but light.
                  We listen.

South Dakota

I cannot push the water anymore.
We beat the waves with our oars
and my face turns pale and warm.
        In our cove beyond the other boats,
            you make a house with sticks
                    and a blanket. I cook
        spaghetti with dark water.
Our fire smells of cedar blue flames
circling the snapping wood.

When I waken, I feel drunk
            and moist. I slip
                from my sleeping bag
            to stand in the morning air.
White mist rests on the lake below me.
        Trees stand along the bank
        crooked and not quite full.
These are cottonwoods. Their swirling leaves
        imprecise and flirtatious. I do not call you
                    to join me.

A blue heron rises from the cliff
      opens its great wings and lopes
            into the gray sky.
I watch until it disappears into the mirage
          of morning.
Sea gulls somewhere circle and screech.

A chill creeps across my body:
      I feel as if I've never been naked before
      that this lake had never lain quiet,
      that this heron was born the day before
      when we climbed up to the pine cliffs
      and watched the carp hover near the shore.

The lights across the water are gone now.
      They hiss at the fog around them.
      The cottonwoods are children, thirty of forty
          whispering to me.
I cannot grasp them. I open my arms to catch the sky
      I raise up and up. The earth shifts beneath my feet
      It does not free me but leaves
      the beating of wings inside my chest.

Etel Adnan

Born and raised in Lebanon, Etel Adnan studied philosophy at the University of California–Berkeley and Harvard. Her novel about Lebanon's civil war, *Sitt Marie Rose*, originally written in French, is considered a classic of Middle Eastern literature and has been translated into several languages. Her poetry, too, has received worldwide attention and garnered her a reputation as a "visionary." At once "deeply personal and political," her poems "explore fissures within words as places where thought enters" and attempt to make sense of the disorder and chaos of the world's many upheavals. In addition to writing poetry and fiction, Adnan is also a major painter and playwright. A frequent traveler to Europe and the Arab world, she lives in Sausalito, California.

from Transcendence

. . . .
2.

The distillation
of reality
the filtering
the cleaning out

the clearing
the pushing aside
the shadow's advance
the revolving of
        thoughts
in the flesh
in the burn
the cut
the bruise and
the amputation

In a day like
this
the body loses
its integrity
and soldiers
while raped
curse the goddesses of
fertility
in a day,
in this day,
time loses its
value on the
market-place as in
this room
this petrified
forest,
this illegitimate
piece of wood,
this chair,
these nails,
this wind,
this stupor.

3.

and in a day
like this
we read assassination
and blood runs
out of mouths
out of minds

we hear cries
over the telephone

we don't see
tears
we don't see
eyes
it's a matter
of what we
hear
of contamination
of knowledge learned
in spare time
and fingernails
bitten
and desires
beaten down
and shame running
down
our
legs

And here comes
despair filling
the refrigerator
and here comes
the ocean   now
a stranger
and the police
get wet
and we shout
through the wood's
thickness
the roof
the basement

no-exit for
the waiting
the terror
the soiled love
and the news replacing
the rain.

4.

I will not
buy bread
not allow the
light in
nor watch
a game by
satellite

I will not
wipe my face
with a soft
towel

I will ask you:

have you paid
your dues
to uneven numbers
have you counted
the corpses

have you told
your doctor
you wish he were
a witch

and warned your veins
not to fool around
with your brain?

Have you measured
the coastline
full of vicious
refugees
did you fear
their power over
you
did you take out
your gun
out of the closet,
from under your
mattress
have you silenced
their voice
their smile
their footsteps
their stench?

at least
did you sleep well?

. . . .

9.

There's murder
in the air
where else?

children
henceforth

not of the earth
are waiting
to become
ashes

To a day
like this one
which is
passing by
there's no
adjustment

rage
exhausted and
following a
cortège
no longer
is contained in
a closed fist
but is feeding
innumerable reservoirs
along the natural
bend of
the mind

It's too early
to rise
still
though undecisive
the sun is piercing
the enlarged circle of
the chorus of
clouds

it has vengeance
in reserve.

. . . .

12.

I have to give
voice
to those
immured
mere
vibrations
but a word is
first atom of
language
bomb
of the dis-
armed
all ending
in ruins
there
for a moment
long moments of
momentous
happenings
in the
sky
the sky
the fullmoon
is treason
but I have
to tell

to those waiting
for their state
a state of
transcendence
have to tell
they're waiting!
they're used to waiting
have to tell them
that I'm enjoying
myself
—I have to reassure them—
because
they are
dying.

from The Arab Apocalypse

I

A yellow sun   A green sun   a yellow sun   A red sun   a blue sun

a [symbol] sun   A sun [symbol]   a [symbol] blue   red [symbol] red   a [symbol] blue

a blue yellow sun a yellow red sun a blue green sun a

a yellow boat a yellow sun a [symbol] red a [symbol]   red blue and yellow

a yellow morning on a green sun a flower flower on a blue blue but

a yellow sun A green sun a yellow sun A red sun a blue sun

a [symbol] yellow A sun [symbol] a small craft [symbol] a boat [symbol]   red   blue

a quiet blue sun on a card table a red which is blue and a wheel

A solar sun a lunar sun a starry sun a nebular sun

A yellow sun   A green sun a yellow sun Qorraich runner ran running

A blue sun before a red sun   a green sun before a lunar sun

A floral sun [symbol]   a small craft as round as a round sun [symbol]   A solar moon

Another sun jealous of Yellow enamoured of Red terrified by Blue horizontal

A sun romantic as Yellow jealous as Blue amorous as a cloud

A frail sun a timid sun [symbol]   vain sorrowful and bellicose sun

A Pharaonic [symbol] boat an Egyptian sun a solar universe and a universal sun

A solar arrow crosses the sky An eye dreads the sun the sun is an eye

A tubular sun haunted by the tubes of the sea [symbol] a sun pernicious and vain

A [symbol] Hopi a Red Indian sun an Arab Black Sun a sun yellow and blue

a solar Hopi a solar Indian reddening a solar Arab darkening
a solar cord a musical Greek a rosace ⚏ solar a sun in an old sky
a sun in the room a room ▣ in a ◗ sun rolling on the sky
a blue sky for a ▣ yellow sun a yellow sky for ⇄⇢ a blue sun
a blue tattoo in the sky ☽ a sun tattooed with sins   solar sins
a Bedu sunstruck a   sun-sick and the sea drowing the sea
a sun alarmed alarming the color yellow the yellow alarming sun moon and sea
a militant tattoo a militant sun in a warm ⟩⟩ universe ⅋ a straight sun
a solar craft under the Nile the Nile crossing a sun the sun laughing
a solar imbecile a lunar cloud a polar woman a sun ultra brave
a ⚡ sun solar nocturnal fluvial bestial choleric and yellow as yellow
an egg yolk sun confined to an asylum tearing its skin into lightning
a solar craft under the Nile the Nile crossing a sun the sun ⬤ laughing
a sunlike and solar tattoo is an Arab eye in the middle of the Milky Way
A ⚡ maddeningly yellow another peacefully green a blue terror   O moon!
A yellow and quiet sun on a quiet and soft horizon next to flowers. Everyday
A sun victory of the yellow on the green of the green ⚘ over the yellow in
the meadow of tears.

. . . .

III

The night of the non-event. War in the vacant sky. The Phantom's absence.
Funerals. Coffin not covered with roses. Unarmed population. Long.
The yellow sun's procession from the mosque to the vacant Place. Mute taxis.
Plainclothed army. Silent hearse. Silenced music. Palestinians with no Palestine.

The night of the Great Inca did not happen. Engineless planes. Extinguished sun.
Fishermen with no fleet fish with no sea fleet with no fish sea without fishermen
Guns with faded flowers Che Guevara reduced to ashes. No shade.
The wind neither rose nor subsided. The Jews are absent. Flat tires.
The little lights are not lit. No child has died. No rain
I did not say that spring was breathing. The dead did not return.

The mosque has launched its unheeded prayer. Lost in the waves.
The street lost its stones. Brilliant asphalt. Useless roads. Dead Army.
Snuffed is the street. To shut off the gas. Refugees with no refuge no candle.
The procession hasn't been scared. Time went by.   Silent Phantom.

Stagnant tide. Weightless blackness. Motionless cold around a non-existent fire. Car with no driver Achrafieh-Hamra words under lock. Fear with no substance. Windowless walled City. A dead man forced to go home on foot. A bullet in the belly.

Prayer in the mosque. Black procession tinier than ants. Allahu Akbar.
Cybernetics of Doom broken machine. A breeze but no garden.
The much awaited enemy has not come. He ate his yellow sun and vomited.
Time: lemon crushed by a wheel grating under funerals
Between Beirut and Sidon there is the sea. This night is not of war.
Nothing is crushed by the Silence. Guns are rusting in travel bags. Revolution.

VII

A warring sun in Beirut thunderous April cool breeze on the ships
yellow sun on a pole an eye in the gun's hole a dead from Palestine
a purple sun in my friend's pocket meanderings in PARIS
a bird on a dead Palestinian's toe a fly at the butchery
Beirut-sulphuric-acid STOP the Quarantina is torching its inmates STOP Beirut
a sun on the finger a sun in the gut a sun climbing an elephant
cannibal anthropophagus sun wart on the cargoes ! ! ! !
a yellow sun on the face cancer on the Palestinian cruelty of the palm tree
I led a ship under the sea to the living and the dead yes yes yes
a black sun 45 black corpses for a single coffin black eye listening
I saw a hawk eat a child's brain in the dumps of Dekouaneh

A dead sun was a toy in Sabra   I cut the sky in two

a sun rotten and eaten by worms floats over Beirut   silence is sold by the pound

Bedouins covered by sarcophagi know that a tattooed moon floods you with dynamite!

the sun blown-up a child blown-up a fish blown-up the street blown-up
eat and vomit the sun eat and vomit the war hear an angel explode

a bestial sun crawls on my backbone and gnaws at my neck. Its hair . . . .
Its hair is falling Outside fascism dressed in green masturbates its guns

O backfired adventure! I saw Beirut-the-fool write with blood Death to the moon!

A rocket shatters the house. Bullets fly. They rip up a store. They stampede a cat

I took the sun by the tail and threw it in the river. Explosion. BOOM . . . .

Beirut syphilis carrying whore   the sun is contaminated by the city

a blue sun receding a Kurd killing an Armenian an Armenian killing a Palestinian . . . .
the solar wheel of Syrian races O insane nomads drinkers of dust
a hydrophilic sun a hilarious yellow sun red and vain red sun
Beirut-the-Mean a Party drunk with petroleum militia in whirlpools

a sun in a belly full of vegetables a system of fat tuberosis a sun which is SOFT

the eucalyptus are in bloom. the Arabs are under the ground. the Americans on the moon.

the sun has eaten its children   I myself was a morning blessed with bliss.

. . . .

XXXIX

When the living rot on the bodies of the dead
When the combatants' teeth become knives
When words lose their meaning and become arsenic
When the aggressors' nails become claws
When old friends hurry to join the carnage
When the victors' eyes become live shells
When clergymen pick up the hammer and crucify
When officials open the door to the enemy
When the mountain peoples' feet weigh like elephants
When roses grow only in cemeteries
When they eat the Palestinian's liver before he's even dead
When the sun itself has no other purpose than being a shroud

the human tide moves on . . .

. . . .
LVIII

Oil wells will dry out and eight-headed monsters will crawl on Earth
neither the cross of David nor the star   will resist the yellow waves
yellow is the color of plague yellow is the sun's color
palm trees will fall in front of the electric organs
the banners of death float on the pylons
the desert will be covered with concrete springs sequestered by angels carrying blue swords
mountains of ice will melt in a boiling sea of salt
people's tongues will turn into tongues of fire
on the Throne of Goodness there will be a mute-deaf
in the seat of Evil we shall install an old mummy
throats will choke with gold iron safes used as coffins
And rats will inherit the Heralded Kingdom.

Saladin Ahmed

Saladin Ahmed was born in Detroit, Michigan, raised in neighboring Dearborn (home to the largest Arab American community in the United States), and educated at the University of Michigan and Rutgers University. His lineage is Lebanese, Egyptian, and Irish, and his poetic influences, evident in the eclecticism and multiplicity of voices found in his work, range from *One Thousand and One Arabian Nights* to the Qur'an, surrealism, the Black Arts Movement, hip-hop, and fantasy novels. His poems have appeared in many anthologies and journals, among them *Post Gibran: Anthology of New Arab American Writing*. He holds an M.F.A. from Brooklyn College and is a Ph.D. candidate in eighteenth-century British literature.

Ghazal

The dark side of green Venus hovers above paper;
there are tides and tidal waves in a soul made of paper.

I could run into the rain-streaked morning, do a handstand
on another man's property, make a friend of paper.

At 1 A.M. in Central Booking two dudes barter
quietly through bars, one of them dangling a dove paper.

Falasteen! They've got you surrounded, subtracting you with
assault choppers while down your raw throat they shove paper!

The myths of then vs. the myths of now—Salah Al-Din,
the general that bitch-slapped Europe, was known to love paper.

Over the Phone, One of Our Hero's Close Personal Homeboys Recounts Life in a College Town

I miss having you around too, dawg.
Listen to my wack-ass routine:
The Great Hand makes a striking motion,
and the day is cracked open,
sliding onto the blazing iron of the world.

I imagine myself as the yellow center:
inconstant, supple and relaxed
until forced to harden against
the whiteness that surrounds me,
the encroaching blank.

The Third World Werewolf Speaks to Our Hero of Life in the Financial Zone

In a word, brother, it is dangerous—
Silver is too easy to come by in this country,
and they confuse the moon with lasers and smog.
But even a half-man has to make a living.
I will have to hide among them until the time is right—
I'll have to hide, one-eyebrowed,
a computer folded beneath my arm.

Ibn Sina

He sits in a blue kaftan like a small ocean
His hand a fierce brown bird—
or like that of a fierce brown bird
It moves from right to left, his calligraphy brush
switching, the snipped mustache of a djinn

Incense burns in a tiny iron cage,
and there are apples at his elbow

Is he writing on versification, jurisprudence,
medicine, remedies of the heart?
Which of his hundred books is he completing?
How can he be so calm, hearing the bombs fall
on his family, only a thousand years away?

Kazim Ali

Kazim Ali is the author of two poetry books, *The Far Mosque* and *The Fortieth Day*, and a novel, *Quinn's Passage*. His poems have been described as "musical" and "metaphysical," bringing "discontinuity to the rapid shifts of postmodern disjunction." Through a mixture of "painterly minimalism, open-field technique and Near Eastern traditions," he revives "the mythological power in things." A former member of the Cocoon Modern Dance Company, Ali has written extensively about poetry and teaches at Oberlin College and the University of Southern Maine.

The Black Madonna at Chartres

The virgin's coat is wood polished black as obsidian stone.

Mary, daughter of Anna, black as stone.

Beaten the veil of Mary paper-thin.

Who I am.

Who I once was.

Wrapped in the veil of the virgin.

Age into stone.

Beneath even this the crypt.

Beneath even that the stone.

Journey

The wind over open water: sharp howling.

Guitar strings breaking.

Solstice having passed days longer now.

Beach aria.

Synaptic dysfunction or syntactic exuberance.

A small figure on the deck looking out across the blue-black.

The years since then drunk and unforgiving.

Wild roses crawl through the rough plank balcony.

Drinking bitter coffee on the terrace.

Weeks after that, alone in the vast public square.

Watching the crowds board the night boat back to the mainland.

Years later another journey you won't take.

Where will you now journey.

For a day.

Sounds of water.

You will sometime soon say: *I am coming home now.*

And not mean it.

What in your life have you meant.

A little inn perched in the hills above Calvi.

The cloud-sheathed cold.

Cold falling into the steep streets of the city.

You are still there.

Tissue-clouded moon swells above the blue-black.

A terse, obscene, spattering of stars.

A blue stone, fastened with a leather strap, cold against your chest.

Closing your eyes at the beach, listening to the rocks being piled,
softly clacking against one another.

Another music for you.

Will you fall?

The wind presses against the portholes.

They rattle slightly in the night.

Rolling sound of rain pouring into the sea.

Wreaking the sound against sleep.

Waking with the light, the drunken year sinking.

The Year of Summer

You came down from the mountains to the shore with your father's voice ringing in your ears, saying over and over again the call to prayer.

The stairs leading down to the water are cracked and marked by awakening.

Awakening in the south the morning sun shines lemon yellow for eleven months, the leaves of the trees telling a book of eleven dreams.

In this book, the sky is sometimes lavender. In this book are colors like you have never seen before.

In this book is the taste of white peach.

The blue-black sea turns milky under the noon-sun.

In the twelfth dream your father is saying your name kindly and gently, whispering into each of your folded ears.

In the year of summer you came south into a city of yellow and white, and what was told of this city was told in trees, and then in leaves, and then in light.

Gallery

You came to the desert, spirit-ridden
illiterate, intending to starve

The sun hand of the violin carving through space
the endless landscape

Acres of ochre, the dust-blue sky, or the stranger,
casually surveying the room

The young man beside you is peering carefully into "The Man Who
                    Taught William Blake Painting In His Dreams"

You are thinking: *I am ready to be touched now, ready to be found*

He is thinking: *How lost, how endless I feel this afternoon*

When will you know: all night: sounds

Violet's brief engines

The violin's empty stomach resonates

Music is a scar unraveling itself in strings

An army of hungry notes shiver down the four strings' furrow

You came to the desert intending to starve   so starve

Assef Al-Jundi

Although he is the son of an accomplished Syrian poet, Assef Al-Jundi did not begin writing poetry until moving to the United States. His poems have appeared in numerous anthologies, including *Poetic Voices without Borders, Inheritance of Light, Between Heaven and Texas,* and *The Spaces between Our Footsteps: Poems and Paintings from the Middle East.* Born in Syria, Al-Jundi lives in San Antonio, Texas.

Flying

The first time I flew, I was seventeen.
In Syria, you take the taxi when you travel.
You go to the taxi garage and wait
until enough passengers fill one for your distant destination.

Two to Hama. We need two more to Hama.
The garage hustler would shout
on the sidewalk.

Even when my father and I traveled
to Amman and Beirut
for my student visa to the U.S.
we took a taxi.
The American Embassy in Damascus
was closed
after The Six Day War.
I don't remember, anymore, why one embassy was not enough,
but they had us travel to Lebanon and Jordan
multiple times. Interviews at each stop

to insure I did not intend to stay.
That I had means of support.
That I had a family that wanted me back after graduation.
That my father owned a piece of land
in Salamieh he could sell
to fly me back home.

In the taxi, I felt hot air blow against my face.
I experienced bumps in the road,
learned the distinctive odor of sheep
as they scurried across dusty roads
with their brands of bright
red, purple and yellow dyes.
I studied the shapes
of rocks. Examined
sun-beaten faces
of villagers on their donkeys.

As the plane sped down
the runway
I thought I was in a huge taxi
until the road stopped.

My family.
Houses.
Fields.
Damascus.
Everything shrank
and blew away.

Clouds were strange billowy animals,
and I wondered what America looked like.

Nostalgic

Sisters and I sitting around a crate of ripe apricots,
pitting them for Mother's jam,
laughing with juice-glazed lips.
How we could not resist
eating more than we put aside.

Proud boy of eleven posing,
arms crossed,
big grin in shorts and new
white shoes and socks.

Mada at curious three
brandished a defiant look
she now keeps in her purse.

Me marching with the Boy Scouts
in the Syrian mountains.
Our leader up front.
Dusty pebbles under my steps.

Mutaa, Ghassan and Maurice
my best high school friends, Damascus.
Uniforms, boots and the nature of God.
I never got to talk to the girls on the balcony.
Mutaa claimed he did.

I took this picture of baby Mona
sitting on a cushion

in Uncle Fareed's tiled yard in Homs.
Now she has two kids of her own.

Making French Fries in that funny inverted boat paper hat
at Burger Chef on Lamar Street in Austin.
A man used to buy cooked meat patties only,
For the dog, he would always say.

Mother young and good-looking.
The smiles on my sisters' faces.
First kiss.
Love.
Lovers.
The white 1962 Buick LaSabre, automatic
with air conditioning.

Apprentice

There is a restlessness in me
that gets worse when I rest.

When I told you
I have been practicing
your art of disappearing,
you smiled excitedly,
said something,
then disappeared.

I sit in a chair that is not there
and fall to the ground.

Alise Alousi

Alise Alousi was born in 1965, her mother from Detroit, her father from Baghdad. Both places continue to influence her life and writings, in ways both imaginable and unimaginable. Alousi studied literature and creative writing at Wayne State University and spent a summer at the Naropa Institute's Jack Kerouac School of Disembodied Poetics. Her poems have appeared in several anthologies, including *Abandon Automobile, I Feel a Little Jumpy,* and *Poets against the War.* She is the author of an early chapbook, *Wearing Doors Away,* and is at work on a full-length collection, *What to Count.* For the past sixteen years, she has worked with children and teens, most recently as a writer-in-residence in the Detroit public schools.

Lipstick

for the siblings

I. Cherries in the Snow

Imagine the snow like
sand it stings
your teeth when
you bite something soft
and it is really hard
to catch blood
dripping from your chin.

II. Crushed Candy

Honeysuckle pinched
ding-dong ditch
neighbor's handprints
ring the small one's neck.

III. Eternal Petal

Every part
of the circle
needs one
move your hand
or the paper
as you go.

Mayfly

for esme

You have the right to
be delicate, transparent
yet still
flatten yourself against
the strong current

appear as if
you're caught in mid-swarm
when you are singularly

flying toward the light.

What to Count

What does it mean to hold your mouth to another's ear. What does it mean to make something stealth. Where do you feel it. Where do things happen when they happen on a train.

A shelter that falls in on itself. A hospital that can't help you, a pencil without lead. Are there things you could use.

A whisper what does it excite in you. She said stand on the corner with a sign should I? Something falling soft in the air tiny disappear your skin damage with a capsule. It is a good way to eat all the time. He doesn't want the numbers in the bag—100.150.200.250.300. Women, children, the old only.

What matters is that you are innocent when you die like this.

Step into the flash. Remember this day. Don't throw rice for the birds, a bubble you catch in your teeth. Smile's not right. The scent behind your ear makes his head hurt.

Sent home crying when the visitors came through hands in pockets and chewing gum and pencils and penicillin and. taking notes. Bombs dropped last week didn't they? In the schoolyard. Where are your dual-use shoes.

What counts is the circle when you dance like this.

Up out of the water too much chlorine in the backyard pool, see it in their eyes. Children. Looking into the sun. What is on the other side.

They say we can't fill the order not even one drop on a hot stone. Nothing will be clean or white again. The x-ray of your wrist, chest, lungs will be done by hand, come back in seven hours. There are too many young men they will die of general malaise right in the street and there is one ambulance in the city and there is nowhere for it to take you.

What counts when you fall like this is the way they lift you bending at the knees.

Lynndie's Other Voice*

An ancient symbol,
eye in the palm, hypnotizing
from a Three Stooges rerun—
what I knew of these parts
before I arrived to a prison,
already bad history
behind its walls.

All the men's eyes looked the same,
black and dull as the dogs they feared.
There "some things stay in the house"
meant a secret, not an animal,
a leash we kept on the wall
camera-ready.

How does a bad idea keep going—
you know something, see
something, a knife out of a drawer
on the wrong night,
matches near bone-dry trees.

Tolerance had little room. We were all just bodies,
some on top, some on bottom.

We called it training. The fence was invisible,
guidelines never given. Torture pure
not simple. You could have asked me
what day it was, who my friends were,
I didn't know. They were all the same,
until they weren't.

It's hard for you to believe,
I'm not the woman you saw
doing those things. She is the dirt
I was born into, but not the fruit
from my tree.

When I have my child,
I will not name him
in regret or sorrow, from false love or
secrets held. I will call him
for the miracle he is
to have come from this
nothing else.

*Lt. Lynndie England was six months pregnant at the time of sentencing for her role in
the torture of Iraqi prisoners at Abu Ghraib.

Nuar Alsadir

Nuar Alsadir's poems "are a delicate mix of the quotidian and the profound. In witty, vibrant, always surprising turns, she reveals to us the weight of each fleeting moment." Widely published in such journals as *Slate, Ploughshares,* the *Kenyon Review, Grand Street,* and *AGNI,* as well as various anthologies, Alsadir teaches writing at New York University, where she also earned an M.F.A. in creative writing and a Ph.D. in literature. A graduate of Amherst College, she has been awarded writing fellowships from Yaddo, the MacDowell Colony, and the Fine Arts Work Center in Provincetown, and her essays have appeared in the *New York Times Magazine, Bookforum,* and *Tin House.*

Bats

They live inside walls—not like you
or the other rodents, but with wings

and fangs, a clicking almost flamenco.
And unlike you, they are not ashamed:

they share their darkness like a piece
of delight and when the circling begins

do not feel their minds invert.
You, crawlers, guard your flight,

may swim the air in dreams
but always rise for breath, belief.

The bats do not need applause.
If you clap, they will change direction.

The Riddle of the Shrink

It is the distress of losing a ticket
or any other document granting passage.

When the phone disconnects
just as you were about to be let in

on a secret, you become the letter
that never receives a response, the ball

that rolls under the neighbor's fence and stays.
The friend you have entrusted with your death

song, an editor, has changed the words.
Now it is you, not your modifiers,

who will dangle, suspended between this world
and the next. The image of the future

is the memory of the dream in which
you are standing before a kiosk, attempting

a transaction with a forgotten code.
The more you talk, the more you are left alone.

At times, you are curious whether or not
someone is in the room, but fear it would be

too revealing to check. At times, you strain
to hear another's conversation while feigning

involvement in your own. When the subway doors
open and everyone rushes to take a seat,

you are trying to get over to the right lane
in fast traffic. It is like wearing stockings

with a stretched-out waistband under a skirt,
or dreaming that the alarm is about to go off.

The Garden

There is no garden, there never was.
The man who cuts the grass is stealing,

making promises with his Miracle-Gro
and reeling in the fish. I want to believe

in something: each morning I look out
at the patches, squint until they turn green.

Are you with me, wherewithal?
I am everywhere without.

A garden is a mood: this one less
of disciple's brood than drought.

Sinan Antoon

Sinan Antoon studied literature at Baghdad University before moving to the United States after the 1991 Gulf War. He earned degrees in Arab studies at Georgetown and Arabic literature at Harvard. Antoon is the author of two poetry books, *The Baghdad Blues* and *A Prism: Wet with Wars*, and a novel, *I`jam*, and his poems, essays, and translations have appeared in publications throughout the Arab and English-speaking world, as well as in German, French, Italian, and Bosnian/Croatian translations. In 2003, as a member of InCounter Productions, he returned to his native Baghdad to codirect and produce the documentary *About Baghdad*, exploring the lives of Iraqis in post-Saddam occupied Iraq. A contributing editor to *Banipal* and a member of the editorial committee of *Middle East Report*, Antoon is currently an assistant professor at New York University.

Wrinkles: on the wind's forehead

1

the wind is a blind mother
stumbling
over the corpses
no shrouds
save the clouds
but the dogs
are much faster

2

the moon is a graveyard
for light
the stars women
wailing

3

the wind was tired
from carrying the coffins
and leaned
against a palm tree
A satellite inquired:
Whereto now?
the silence
in the wind's cane murmured:
"Baghdad"
and the palm tree caught fire

4

the soldier's fingers scrape
and scrabble
like question marks
or sickles
they search the womb
of the wind
for weapons
. . .
nothing but smoke
and depleted uranium

5

how narrow is this strait
which sleeps
between two wars
but I must cross it

6

My heart is a stork
perched on a distant dome
in Baghdad
its nest made of bones
its sky
of death

7

This is not the first time
myths wash their face
with our blood
(t)here they are
looking in horizon's mirror
as they don our bones

8

war salivates
tyrants and historians pant
a wrinkle smiles
on the face of a child
who will play
during a break
between wars

9

The Euphrates
is a long procession
Cities pat its shoulders
as palm trees weep

10

The child plays
in time's garden
but war calls upon her
from inside:
come on in!

11

The grave is a mirror
into which the child looks
and dreams:
when will I grow up
and be like my father
. . .
dead

12

the Tigris and Euphrates
are two strings
in death's lute
and we are songs
or fingers strumming

13

For two and a half wars
I've been here
in this room
whose window is a grave
that I'm afraid of opening
there is a mirror on the wall
when I stand before it

naked
my bones laugh
and I hear death's fingers
tickling the door

14

I place my ear
on the belly of this moment
I hear wailing
I put it on another moment:
—the same!

A Photograph

*(Of an Iraqi Boy on the Front Page
of the New York Times)*

he sat
at the edge of the truck
(eight or nine years old?)
surrounded by his family:
his father,
mother,
and five siblings
were asleep
his head was buried
in his hands
all the clouds of the world
were waiting
on the threshold of his eyes
the tall man wiped off the sweat
and started digging
the seventh grave

A Letter

Silently
I address them
The dead Iraqis
Where do we stand now?
Give or take a few hundred thousands?
. . . .
Had you been birds,
your disappearance might have caused some outrage
You could have flown en masse
over a metropolis,
clouded its skies for a few hours
in protest.
Meteorologists and bird-watchers
surely would have noticed
Had you been trees,
you would have made a beautiful forest
whose destruction would have been deemed a crime
against the planet.
Had you been words,
you would have formed a precious book
or manuscript whose loss
would be mourned across the world
But you are none of these
And you had to pass quietly and uneventfully
No one will campaign for you
No one cares to represent you
No absentee ballots have been issued or sent
You will have to wait decades
for a monument,
or a tiny museum.

If you are lucky
in provoking retroactive guilt
your names will be inscribed on a wall somewhere
But until then, you may welcome more to your midst
and form a vast silent chorus
of ghosts,
condemning the spectators and the actors.
Exeunt Omens!

Delving

The sea is a lexicon
of blueness
assiduously read
by the sun
your body, too
is a lexicon
of my desires
its first letter
will take a lifetime!

Sifting

my eyes
are two sieves
sifting
in piles of others
for you

Walid Bitar

Walid Bitar was born in Beirut in 1961, spent his childhood there, and later immigrated with his family to Canada. His poems, collected in *Maps with Moving Parts, 2 Guys on Holy Land, Bastardi Puri,* and *The Empire's Missing Links,* are often "torn between the comic and the inconsolable," exploring "the conflicts and tensions inherent at the intersection of traditional Western modes of thought with modern geopolitical realities." He has traveled and taught in Asia, Europe, and North America, most recently teaching English at Lebanese American University.

Looking You in the Back of the Head

I'll compare you to the outskirts of Copenhagen,
I'll compare you to a swan made of twisted
coat-hangers, to Mars, to a toad, to pink
gum stretched from the pavement by a clog, to a rose,
a mailman's uniform, the Klondike Goldrush,
popcorn spilled on a black velvet purse,
an alligator, a sky blue bongo drum,
a pomegranate with many cavities, a pine nut,
an unsigned income tax return, I'll compare
you to a pear, an avocado, I don't care
as long as after all is said and done
it wasn't you I was talking about—let all
these comparisons be so much confetti decking out
the cathedral of amnesia which, by the way,
is not a cathedral at all, it's a labyrinth,
a celebration, onion soup, a mallard, and yes
I'm happy the neighbors love us very much
because they're gulls made of swans made of twisted

coat-hangers, and all my clothes are on the floor, and I'm—
naked? No, this is not my body—*you're* naked;
get away from my clothes; I love those clothes!
From now on you do what I do, you are me,
not you at all—I'll do what you like, like plantains,
like apple pie, double digit inflation, and then baboons.
In return, repeat after me: I. Now it's your turn: "I."

Survival of the Fittest

Our ancestors wouldn't know what to make
of us if they were here; we're their immortality,
which they may enjoy at heavenly stages,
but back down in this bombed-out city

we're cannon and fodder for sight's artillery.
Light isn't reflected off objects into us.
We fire the world out of our sockets, real
only in so far as demigods we trust

say so. We wait for news and entertain
ourselves by sampling our favourite scams:
selling the auctioneer's tongue as it auctions,
clapping with our earrings instead of our hands . . .

We're not an audience for opening nights.
We interrupt actors because we're bored
and angry enough to rewrite their lines.
Our idea of socializing is to forge

one another's signatures at struggle meetings
modeled on Maoist peasant scenes,

except that now we pull enough strings.
The self-criticism of each human being

describes foreign bodies—a hippopotamus,
or the sun with its repetitive rising and falling
valuable as a gold mine immune to rushes,
or, in my case, the Loch Ness monster.

I'm restless at rest, though when in motion
longing for stasis. So I've found a compromise
and become a figment not of my imagination,
but of somebody else's. That's how one survives

after he's gone, and I'll be leaving soon.
The neighbours are trick-or-treating. I'm out
of the usual candy—give them ships of fools,
laws of hospitality on automatic pilot.

Here's my strategy: I'll welcome them into
my study, the drawers and the garbage pails
that are spilled, jumped on, occasionally hurled
across the floor we mop up for stage names

fit for a tomb. If we sleep at the wheels
of post-Darwinian worlds, our survival
means manic rehearsals and depressing revivals
of agnostic takes on the Lazarus theme.

Progress Report

We waited for news; we were old-fashioned,
and didn't realize our patience was futile.
We live in an age whose executions and trials
are kept well away from the three dimensions,

away from time even—justice is eternal.
And so, for some reason, are our criminals.
At least that's what we're told in the papers:
no more arrests, and no more judges.

Here's to stereotypical searches,
poking the mind with asinine fingers,
to equality's rectums (his and hers).
Who can tell the coppers from the nurses?

I couldn't care less about human judgment,
including my own. Any point of view,
the hired libeler's, or the lawsuit's,
is a foreigner with a laughable accent.

Still, there have been days I regret
when wars that were raging excluded my causes.
Rounds of ammunition punctuated my pauses.
I made my living correcting a grammar

I had no faith in. At Teacher's Lounge,
a bordello near campus, at Hotel Arhaba
(the sign lost its M), in flocks of truths and lies,
the black sheep behaved just like the whites.

Unlike a priest, when I adjusted my collar,
it had no meaning for this congregation

whose *Weltanschauung,* like nuclear fission's,
was so worldly it blew off all the others.

Many, too many, of these wasted perspectives
glide now over our scarecrow Bastille
without any instinct to set us free.
Revolution is air—they're insouciant birds.

and so, at most, can be recreated.
How do they help us, all our frescoes,
always earthbound, inevitably argot?
We'll never speak the language of a court.

A Disposition of the Antiquities

You know how it is with dictators and flunkies . . .
get as many citizens as possible involved
in the jack-of-all-trades firing squads,
Jills too, divers ages, creeds, ethnicities . . .

That way, with guilt, it's share and share alike.
But why serve up so jam-packed an idea?
We need something we can empty, an ear:
when chips are down, it's easiest to bribe

with babble about it being a roulette wheel.
Words are a ball in no-man's land,
especially mispronounced by shifting sands,
museums trashed, bronze poses effete,

withdrawn from a 5,000-year-old account,
the Mesopotamian. A new world forwards

open-hearted tips of the hat to feudal
and space-age under-the-table body counts

whose survivors we ask how all went, looking away
to focus on nothing in particular, the distance
resettled by the usual heroines and princes,
a landscape to some, to others eternity

but to this boy more of our enemy's gold.
Yes, we occupy what we meditate on,
frame, without painting, a scene with our brawn
lest something escape us. Our own scent grows cold,

but luckily we didn't come east to search souls,
ours or the locals'. That would be intrusive.
We're here to liberate and barter for the looters'
antiquities—resell them as "postmodern dolls,"

or some other code name we'll come up with
for the black markets that could be called white,
any colour in fact. Why put up a fight
when the opponent is our own rich vocabulary?

Under the Table

The animals we are working to death
can't say if they're suffering. What they feel
has no meaning, and the message this sends
us is any we choose to believe,

a final decision I will make seem
as if arrived at democratically.

While we're arguing, we'll gather steam
for the engine invented retroactively,

consciousness one tricky customer—
by definition, truth isn't on sale,
and yet we buy it over the counter
our dancing midgets place under the table,

tactics passed down through generations
until our expectations are lowered,
and a process of elimination
teaches us it too will soon be over.

In most cases, we overlook details.
Still, there's not much in man so instinctive
it doesn't leave a long paper trail
that is recycled continuously,

the consequences largely unintended,
you claim today, but those of us who
watched you grow saw how you perfected
your blindness working with piano tuners,

and passing judgment gives such great pleasure.
I feel, for a few moments, a rush
proving exactly how powerless
an object of my attention becomes.

Ahimsa Timoteo Bodhrán

Born in the South Bronx in 1974, Ahimsa Timoteo Bodhrán earned an M.F.A. from Brooklyn College and is a Ph.D. candidate in American studies from Michigan State University. This coming together of artistic and critical traditions is echoed in his poetry, which engages and is influenced by the work of women and queer people of color, the most influential being Cherríe Moraga and Gamba Adisa (Audre Lorde). His poems, which have appeared in over eighty journals and anthologies in the United States and abroad, are collected in his forthcoming book, *Yerbabuena/Mala yerba, All My Roots Need Rain.*

Manos .17

*for EL, LC, JR, T, APA, OB, VTTV, MKN,
J, LM, JB, JI, CJ, AS, OM, VR, & MG*

1. fireflies, without holes, jars, in brooklyn, smeared on concrete, glow. straight

   boys and ants. moments stolen before the semester begins. quarter system. a

   big magnifying glass. blighted buck/et of water. crustaceans in a barrel. one limb. left

   hands are not meant for writing. *i want the big one.* tap, tap, against glass. ruler

   against thumb. meant for building sneakers. such fragile leaders. numbed knuckles. nuns

   looking. cooking. cooked children. another fairy tale. good posture and gingerbread fantasies. fixed teeth. tongue clicking. notes. passed. things our parents can't read—

though u.s. born. multi-valence, calle y clase, performativity, ours. raise

the shades. *serenade us.* too much light. lower them. luminarias. peor la raza. pigeon

hapa. pig-din. pork latkes. how they describe us speaking. i love you in 15 week

cycles. to pieces. to pieces. luciérnagas. brief bits of light. we

extinguish. squealing lobsters. butter. toil and trouble. *all a's.*

2. reasonable dragonfly, buzzing as i bathe. neon blue.
   waterfall, overlooking your people's land. tourists.
   roundhouse exit, which way to spin.
   no kicking.
   disrupted ceremony, feathers falling from hair. mis-
   interpreted tradition. bear-proof lockers. (how to get inside?)
   the women in the kitchen. "juice." blessed water. in-
   fidelity. finding my own way, hitching.
   home.

   how you look at children.

   chickasaw riders and diné devotion. a fire dance. cops
   pulling us over. routine inspection. driver's license.
   feather removal. fuzzy dice = a protected species.

   mono(syllable). a kissing dis-ease. no.

3. keep on reminding me. i'm just a drunk. humble drunk.

4. male maps and automatic weapons. kuwait(i refugee). tajweed. how to
   speak to you. recitations. the proper tone. oil field fire. valdez. wildlife
   in alaska not the only ones endangered. the u.s., only one with an envi-

ronment(al movement)? traditional fisherwomen. centricity. may i approach the bima? *tallit to torah. tallit to torah. labios. labios.* muslim-jewish relations. not the first such couple (to spawn). *[breed resentment = hatred of mixed bloods and heterosexuals.]* what some think when i say "arab jewish." mernissi and her queens. an adnan painting, hall cd, cher's daughter. bi invisibility. our points of reference. neither of us is lebanese. that means something (here). sisters who lose interest in you once they learn your race. all respect to the yup'ik and "aleut" people. tlingit and haida too. an indigenous poetics. poets and writers still lists mary tallmountain among the living. a post-humous poetics. tsimshian. guess she is. "save the samoans." our ship(ment) is coming (in). pieces. *you can't say anything write.* requiem. rest.

5. the abandoned temples of memory.

6. meal expensive, something could not afford. momma never worked in a place like this, don't even know if she'd've gotten through the door. (maybe they have another entrance for us.) too much glass in this restaurant, and not enough walls. no prices on the menu. tell me to order whatever i like—you'll pay for it. find the cheapest thing, ask waiter on way to restroom how much he'll cost. return to place order. delicious, artistic, small in portion. want me happy. splayed open. julienned. smattering of coconut. an odd grape. carrot. cannot. twenty-four. years before some thing can digest this meal. amalgym. *a whole day's pay.* and swallow it down.

7. you give them a twenty. crisp edges. clean. "it's the smallest i have." almost forget to ask for change. some kid's gonna eat good tonite.

8. "parking for puerto ricans only."

9. model(s) for hiv (prevent infection). other myths of living. an androgynous nursery rhyme.

nuclear assault. tears. genetic skin. the damage tv does. want you inside me.

peel back my shirt. stop. start again. something you do not want to see. another infomercial.

my bare unformed chest stares back at you. blue glow.

my womanly thighs fall away. ginsu-carved can.

place, lodged at your hips. roll over, go back to sleep. even branches.

a vacuum pump for better packing.

pillow wetter than your sweated sheets. back turned to mine. an upswelling. (de)creases.

yet another nite spent alone in someone else's bed.

10. slapped dark dominos on a table. brown boy party. who ain't on crack? downstairs in basement fucking. too eager. wanna inside without even wet yet. reach for you when in, make sure condom on. oakland and other nightmares. rug burns and concrete scars. a close fade. razor lumps. bittermint. bones.

11. año nuevo, colored celt(s), duplex, directions more than 4. southwest/ northwest, depends on how you look at it. a "native-looking" child from the white side. how we put been to their "ceremonial" purposes. your niece, tell me, she ain't yaqui. how all people look indian after a while.

when dilation appears normal. a brief puff of air. the third line (backwards). again.

what urbanization has done. and the devil's drink/drugs.

dance you into living. sobriedad remix. sin olive.

hope you hear this, above the music.

12. *angels. singing.* the city you are from. plurals.

13. barometers of boyhood.

   locks that free us. an intimacy with caltrain. jealous sheep. what i measure against.

   many generation-ed miscegenation. what jesus must've looked like.

   my summers will always belong to you.

14. a delayed orgasm.

   blue-balled and high yellow, "negro green" is your favorite colour.

   later, i hear from you that you are dating someone mexican. i forget to ask you his skin color.

15. a year after there is no more grocery stores. kristallnacht l.a. *some* myth. can you hang clothes on it?

   sa-i-ku. a kim contextualization. dictée re-issue. am.

   don't date two or more at once, so have to choose. for whatever stupid, fucked-up, internalized, racist reason, i pick him. he ends up raping me. i wonder what you would've been like.

   i would kiss your folded lids, like healing hands, hovering, holding me.

16. your campus, nothing but trees and brown people building shit.

   wonder how long you could get locked up for doing this.

   bumped body parts.

   years later, i will miss the peaked passions of the closet, the way in which everything, all the stakes, are higher.

   guide me through acts which need no guidance. our bodies lead the way.

gapped letters and other corporations. a nation reduced to a cocaine trade. dreidel song. geld. inedible chocolate. the same plant. urine samples. where we go for funding.

your potential success means so much to you. wonder what you'd sell for it.

back rubbing back, front s(m)oothing front, *the original soft-drink*, have had men before you, both white, one high school, the other, with which first colonial contact was made, england, an exchange student i met while in germany while also exchanged over for. in tagalog, the diminutive of your name means "here." but you are not. you were my first love. i cried over you. you were my first.

i have always loved my own dark, queer, and colored jewish kind.

17. we dance. but not as close.

Mint

Prune mint—a large quantity will grow back. Uproot it—some of it will manage to keep a root-hold and return. Put some in water—new roots come forth . . . you can plant it almost anywhere and it will flourish.

—Anne J. M. Mamary

1.

None of our worries are what they seem.

You did not want this way to be wise.
If only the lessons could come more slowly, more easily, with less/more calm.

Who knew we'd be elders at 25.

We have all been weeds, known the pull of a farmer's hands.

Each of us is indigenous somewhere.

Somewhere. Sometimes the graft has taken hold, we have taken their money, it feels like any other drug, limb, necessity; is breathing possible without gills, bills?

As if we all come from someplace singular, without cousins or long winters. Fins.

Where I am from is not only a desert.
Other climes, the micros of the bay.

All our views are poisoned.

2.

This ledge, Lebanese, of Green, overlooking Dolores, the old Mission, cemetery of my ancestors, moved to Buena Vista, headstones, steps for white people to walk on, folks to climb, Christian-like, to the top. *Flag on the moon.* Perhaps a cross will be placed there . . . and the earth bleed.

Here, this place, pillow of chamomile, old cat meowing, rubbing against my leg. Animals and their souls. Sonya.

The "Sephardic" cemeteries of Manhattan, the lower half, lower majority, Spic and Jew, A-rab and African, "Orientals," Black (power), Mizrahim, Colma. All the places my grandfather is not buried.

I have never been to a grave of my own people.

3.

Ice cream. Green with little bits of brown chocolate.
Tea. With lots of honey. A Corelle cup.

Laban, with berries, banana, and this leaf. Zimt.
Pasta, con el primo, al-bahaca.

A York Peppermint Patty. Shivers.
My spine, straightened. A winter wind.

4.

colmar = to fill to the brim.

Colma. "A place that is filled." *With spirits.*

Not all the bodies were moved.

Poltergeist = a ghost that crashes about, is not quiet. Or happy. *Trapped.*

El Presidio.

There are places where nothing grows.
We build houses there.

5.

If only we knew the right prayers to say, songs to sing.
But none of us speak the language anymore.

A Chicano poet keeps on referring to my people in the past tense.
He is drunk.

6.

colmar = to use up one's patience; to fulfill one's destiny; live one's dreams.

To receive positive attention. To be showered with affection. To be an object of pride.

For dying.

colmado = a grocery story.

A place where things can be bought. Or, a place where things are sold.
Bodies. Blocks. Blood.

colmatación = silting.

The way a river is filled, the way water is slowed, and things settle out, become clear, less muddied. The way stone is made.

Or story.

7.

If you were small, I would wrap you in this blanket. I only have a piece of it now, as do you.

Pox-free and brown, it is enough to keep us warm, remind us of home.

You were born into it. And I am now part of your weave.

I would send you clippings from my garden, but I have none.

What to send you? Chipped brick?

Strawberries were the first of the season. I loved to eat them.

As did the rabbits.

8.

Something cool that replaces the fire.

Water. Ash. Mud.

9.

Sometimes, I run my fingers through the chimes of your brother's catcher, feel my face against its feather, count each bead. Its web is a good one. My dreams are peaceful.

I think of you. What we need to say is unspoken, I can see it in your eyes, the hair you cut for me when abuela died, and again when I moved from/to this place. There is green and brown and blue. Hazel.

Something else by which to cool us, sooth us. Calm the body, and close the eyes.

But not forever.

May we always be Sacred. And grow/ing. Full.

10.

Some may think that nothing dwells here, no seed left intact. But we have always looked with more than the naked eye, in(to) the cracked crevasses of the body. *The pollen is on our faces. We are flowers kissing.* We need not their machines to see beauty, know harmony, know the inner workings of the soil and soul/earth.

I greet you on the horizon. We bloom. Our sweetness is everywhere.

You greet me with bits of green in your teeth.
The one place they did not think to look. Tierra.

Hayan Charara

Born in Detroit, Michigan, in 1972, Hayan Charara studied biology and English at Wayne State University in Detroit, cultural theory at New York University, and literature at the University of Houston. His poems are "intensely personal," "hard-bitten and meditative," and possess "a healthy dose of humility and openness to both the wonder and the terror of this world." He strives often to unsettle his readers, compelling them to actively participate in his poems. Widely published in journals and anthologies, including *American Poetry: The Next Generation* and *Present/Tense: Poets in the World*, he is the author of two books, *The Alchemist's Diary* and *The Sadness of Others*, which was nominated for the National Book Award in 2006. For many years, he lived and taught in New York City, and he now makes his home in Texas. He is also a woodworker.

Thinking American

—*for Dioniso D. Martínez*

Take Detroit, where boys
are manufactured into men, where
you learn to think in American.
You speak to no one unless someone
speaks to you. Everyone is suspect:
baldheaded carriers from the post office;
old Polish ladies who swear
to Jesus, Joseph, and Mary;
your brother, especially your brother,
waiting in a long line for work.
There's always a flip side.
No matter what happens,
tomorrow is a day away,
or a gin bottle if you can't sleep,

and if you stopped drinking,
a pack of cigarettes. After that,
you're on your own, you pack up
and leave. You still call
the city beside the strait home.
Make no mistake, it's miserable.
After all, you bought a one-way
Greyhound ticket, cursed each
and every pothole on the road out.
But that's where you stood
before a mirror in the dark,
where you were too tired
to complain. You never go back.
Things could be worse. Maybe.
Detroit is a shithole, it's where
you were pulled from the womb
into the streets. Listen,
when I say Detroit, I mean any place.
By thinking American, I mean made.

Washing My Father

His cupped hands hid the space
between his legs. Droplets,
which hung momentarily
at the lip of the faucet,
plopped into the tub—
the only noise in the bathroom.
Except for his breathing—
the deep inhales of steam
rising from the surface.
Except, too, the water

from a soapy sponge
pressed flat against his back—
the warm trickle
down his flanks.
I washed where
he could barely reach.

When he was ready,
I filled a jug with the bath water
he sat in, poured it over
the nape of his neck,
over his shoulders,
and lastly, over my hands.
I was careful not to dry them
with the towel hung on the knob—
this was his. Gently,
I locked the door behind me,
his back still turned away,
the click thunderous in that quiet.

This is not about pity.
I did not yet know that kind of love.
Nor is it about a son
bathing a father too old
to wash himself.
I was ten years old.
He was a young man.
Plain and simple,
my father made me.
It is what he did.
He never required a reason,
and nobody ever asked why.

Usage

An assumption, *a* pejorative, *an* honest language, *an* honorable
death. In grade school, I refused to *accept* the mayor's
handshake; he smiled at everyone *except* people with names
like mine. I was born here. I didn't have to *adopt* America,
but I *adapted* to it. You understand: a man must be *averse*
to opinions that have *adverse* impacts on whether he lives
or dies. "Before taking any *advice,* know the language
of those who seek to *advise* you." Certain words *affected*
me. Sand nigger, I was called. Camel jockey. What was
the *effect?* While I *already* muttered under my breath,
I did so even more. I am not *altogether* sure we can *all
together* come. Everything was not *all right.* Everything
is not *all right.* Imagine poetry without *allusions* to
Shakespeare, Greek mythology, the Bible; or *allusions*
without the adjectives "fanatical," "extremist," "Islamic,"
"right," "left," "Christian," "conservative," "liberal." /
Language written or translated into a single tongue gives
the *illusion* of tradition. *A lot* of people murder language—
a lot fully aware. *Among* all the dead, choose between
"us" and "them." *Among* all the names for the dead—
mother, father, brother, sister, husband, wife, child, friend,
colleague, neighbor, teacher, student, stranger—choose
between "citizen" and "terrorist." / And poet? *Immoral,*
yes, but never *amoral?* Large *amounts,* the number
between 75 and 90 percent of the estimated 150 million
to 1 billion—civilians—killed during wars, over all of recorded
human history. *Anxious* is "worried" or "apprehensive." /
American poetry, Americans. Young, I learned *anyone*
born here could become President. Older, I can point to
any one of a hundred reasons why this is a lie. *Anyway,*

I don't want to be President, not of a country, or club, not
here or there, not *anywhere*. He said, "I turned the car
around *because* it began raining bombs." There's no chance
of ambiguity—an *as* here could mean "because" or "when";
it makes no difference—he saw the sky, felt the ground,
knew what would come next; it matters little when the heart
rate jumps from 70 to 200 beats per minute in less than
a second. What they did to my grandfather was *awful*—
its wretchedness, awe-inspiring; its cruelty, terrible; it was
awfully hard to forget. Just after 8:46 A.M., I wondered *awhile*
what would happen next. At 9:03 A.M., I knew there was going
to be trouble for *a while* to come. When in her grief,
the woman said, "We're going to hurt them *bad,"* she meant
to say, "We're going to hurt them *badly."* For seventeen days,
during air strikes, my grandfather slept on a cot *beside* a kerosene
lamp in the basement of his house. *Besides* a few days worth
of pills, and a gallon of water, he had nothing else to eat
or drink. Given these conditions, none of us were surprised
that on the eighteenth day, he died. / *Besides,* he was
eighty-two years old. I *can* write what I please. I don't need
to ask, *May* I? Like a song: Men with *capital* meet in
the *Capitol* in the nation's *capital.* Any disagreements,
censored; those making them—poets, dissenters, activists—
censured. The aftermath, approximately 655,000 people killed. /
"The Human Cost of War in Iraq: A Mortality Study, 2002–2006,"
Bloomsburg School of Public Health, Johns Hopkins University
(Baltimore, Maryland); School of Medicine, Al Mustansiriya
University (Baghdad, Iraq); in cooperation with the Center
for International Studies, Massachusetts Institute of Technology
(Cambridge, Massachusetts). The figure just *cited*—655,000
dead—resulted from a household survey conducted at actual *sites,*
in Iraq, not the Pentagon, or White House, or a newsroom,

or someone's imagination. Of *course,* language has been
corrupted. Look, the President, who speaks *coarsely,* says,
"We must stay the *course.*" The problem with "Let your
conscience be your guide" is you must first be aware, *conscious,*
of the fact that a moral principle is a subjective thing. I wonder:
when one "smokes 'em out of a hole," if the person doing
the smoking is *conscious* of his *conscience* at work. / Am I
fully *conscious* of how I arrived at this? The *continual*
dissemination of similar images and ideas. / The *continual*
aired footage of planes striking the towers, the towers
crumbling to the streets, dust, screams, a *continuous* reel
of destruction, fear, as if the attacks were happening twenty-four
hours a day, every day, any time. For a while, I *couldn't*
care less about war. / Then I saw corpses, of boys, who
looked just like me. This was 1982, at age ten. Ever since,
I *couldn't care less* why anyone would want it. In 1982,
any one of those boys *could have* been me. Now, it's any one
of those dead men could be me. The Secretary of State
offered such *counsel* to the ambassadors of the world that
the United Nations Security *Council* nodded in favor of war.
Criterion easily becomes *criteria.* Even easier: to no longer
require either. The *data* turned out false. / The doctrine
of preemption ultimately negated its need. While we both
speak English, our languages are so *different from* each other,
yours might as well be Greek to me. When the black man
in the park asked, "Are you Mexican, Puerto Rican, or are you
Pakistani?" and I said, "I'm Arab," and he replied, "Damn.
Someone *don't* like you very much," I understood perfectly
what he meant. The President alluded to the Crusades because of
(not *due to*) a lack of knowledge. / Later, he retracted the statement,
worried it might offend the Middle East; it never occurred
the offense taken was *due to* the bombs shredding them

to bits and pieces. "You are *either* with us or with the terrorists"
(September 20, 2001). "You're *either* with us or against us"
(November 6, 2001). The day after, the disc jockey
advocated, on air, a thirty-three cent solution (the cost of a bullet)
to the problem of terrorists in our midst—he meant in New York;
also, by terrorists, I wonder, did he know he meant cab drivers,
hot dog vendors, students, bankers, neighbors, passers-by,
New Yorkers, Americans; did he know he also meant Sikhs,
Hindus, Iranians, Africans, Asians; did he know, too,
he meant Christians, Jews, Buddhists, Atheists; did he realize
he was *eliciting* a violent response, on the radio, in the afternoon? /
Among those who did not find the remark at all *illicit*:
the owners of the radio station, the FCC, the mayor, the governor,
members of the House, the Senate, the President of the United States.
Emigrate is better than *immigrate*. Proof: No such thing as
illegal *emigration*. Further proof: *Emigration* is never
an election issue. I heard *enthusiastic* speeches. They hate
our freedoms, our way of life, our this, that, and the other,
and so on (not *etc.*). Not *everyone* agreed *every one* not
"with us" was "against us." Detroit was *farther* from home
than my father ever imagined. / He convinced himself soon after
arriving here he had ventured *further* than he should have.
Fewer people live in his hometown than when he left, in 1966.
The number, even *less*, following thirty-four straight days
of aerial bombardment. *First* (not *firstly*) my father spoke
Arabic; *second* (not *secondly*) he spoke broken English, *third*
(not *thirdly*) he spoke Arabic at home and English at work; *fourth*
(not *fourthly*) he refused to speak English anymore. Not every
poem is *good*. Not every poem does *well*. Not every poem is *well*,
either. Nor does every poem do *good*. "To grow the economy"
is more than jargon. / Can a democracy *grow* without violence?
Ours didn't. / They still plan to *grow* tomatoes this year, despite

what was done. Several men, civilian workers, identified
as enemies, were *hanged* on a bridge, bodies torched, corpses
swaying in the breeze. / Photographs of the dead were *hung*
with care. I can *hardly* describe what is going on. Day after day,
he told *himself,* "I am an American. I eat apple pie. I watch baseball.
I read American poetry. I speak American English. I was born
in Detroit, a city as American as it gets. I vote. I work. I pay taxes,
too many taxes. I own a car. I make mortgage payments. I am not
hungry. I worry less than the rest of the world. I could stand to lose
a few pounds. I eat several types of cuisine on a regular basis.
I flush toilets. I let the faucet drip. I have central air-conditioning.
I will never starve to death or experience famine. I will never die
of malaria. I can say whatever the fuck I please." Even words
succumbed; *hopefully* turned into a kind of joke; *hopeful,* a slur.
However, I use the words, but less, with more care. The President
implied compassion; but *inferred* otherwise. This is not
meant to be *ingenious.* Nor is it *ingenuous.* The more
he got *into* it, the more he saw poetry, like language, was *in*
a constant state of becoming. *Regardless,* or because of this,
he welcomed the misuse of language. Language is *its* own
worst enemy—*it's* the snake devouring *its* own tail. They
thought of us not *kind of* or *sort of* but as *somewhat* American.
Lie: "To recline or rest on a surface"? No. "To put or place
something"? No. Depleted uranium, heavy like *lead; its* use—
uranium shells—*led* to birth defects. When in his anger,
the man said, "We're going to *teach* them a lesson," I wonder
what he thought they would *learn.* In a war, a soldier is
less likely to die than a civilian. He looks *like* he hates
our freedoms. / You don't know them *like* I do. / He looks *as* if
he hates our freedoms. / You don't know them *as* I do.
When in his sorrow, my father said, "Everybody *loose* in war,"
I knew exactly what he meant. It *may be* poets should

fight wars. *Maybe* then, metaphors—not bodies, not hillsides,
not hospitals, not schools—will explode. I *might have*
watched the popular sitcom if not for my family—they were
under attack, they *might have* died. / Others *may have* been
laughing at jokes while bodies were being torn apart.
I could not risk that kind of laughter. Of all the *media*
covering war, which *medium* best abolishes the truth?
I deceive *myself.* / I will deceive you *myself.* In the Bronx,
I *passed* as Puerto Rican. I *passed* as Greek in Queens,
also Brazilian, Pakistani, Bangladeshi, even a famous,
good-looking American movie actor. As Iranian in Manhattan.
At the mall in New Jersey, the sales clerk guessed Italian.
Where Henry Ford was born, my hometown, I always *pass*
as Arab. / I may look like the men in the great paintings
of the Near East, but their lives, their ways, I assure you,
are in the *past. Plus,* except in those paintings, or at the movies,
I never saw Arabs with multiple wives, or who rode camels,
lived in silk tents, drank from desert wells; *moreover,* it's time
to move past that. Did language *precede* violence? / Can
violence *proceed* without language? It broke my father's heart
to talk about the *principle* of equal justice. The news aired
several *quotations* from the airline passengers, one of whom was
a middle-aged man with children, who said, "I didn't feel
safe with them on board." He used the word "them" though
only one, an Arab, was on the plane. Being from Detroit,
I couldn't help but think of Rosa Parks. Then I got angry.
I said to the TV, to no one in particular, "If you don't feel safe,
then you get off the goddamn plane." / You can *quote* me
on that. I was *really* angry—not *real* angry, but *really* angry.
The *reason?* A poet asked me why I didn't write poems
about Muslim and Arab violence against others, and I said I did,
and then he said he meant violence against Americans and Israelis,

respectively, and I said I did, and before I could go on, he interrupted
to ask why I didn't write poems about mothers who sent
their sons and daughters on suicide missions. As if, as if, as if.
I *respectfully* decline to answer any more questions. / Write
your own goddamn poem! Does this poem gratify the physical
senses? Does it use *sensuous* language? It certainly does not
attempt to gratify those senses associated with sexual pleasure.
In this way, it may not be a *sensual* poem. However, men have
been known to experience sexual gratification in situations
involving power, especially over women, other men, life, and
language. My father said, "No matter how angry they make you,
invite the agents in the house, offer them coffee, be polite.
If they stay long, ask them to *sit*. Otherwise, they will try to *set*
you straight." When in his frustration, he said, *"Should of,*
could of, would of," he meant, "Stop, leave me alone, I refuse
to examine the problem further." Because (not *since*) the terrorists
attacked us, we became more like the rest of the world than
ever before. This is *supposed to* be a poem; it is *supposed to*
be in a conversation with you. Be *sure and* participate.
"No language is more violent *than* another," he said. *Then*
he laughed, and said, "Except the one you use." Do conflicts
of interest exist when governments award wartime contracts
to companies *that* have close ties to government officials?
From 1995 to 2000, Dick Cheney, Vice President of the United States,
was CEO of Halliburton, *which* is headquartered in Houston,
Texas, near Bush International Airport. Would they benefit
themselves by declaring war? Please send *those* men back home.
My grandfather lay *there* unconscious. For days, *there* was
no water, no medicine, nothing to eat. The soldiers left *their*
footprints at the doorstep. / His sons and daughters, *they're* now
grieving him. "Try not *to* make *too* much of it" was the advice
given after *two* Homeland Security agents visited my house,

not once, not twice, but three times. I'm *waiting for* my right
mind. The language is a long *ways* from here. After
the bombs fell, I called every night to find out *whether* my father
was alive or dead. He always asked, "How's the *weather* there?"
Soon enough, he assured me, things would return to normal,
that (not *where*) a ceasefire was on the way. *Although*
(not *while*) I spoke English with my father, he replied in Arabic.
Then I wondered, *who's* to decide *whose* language it is anyway—
you, me? *your* mother, father, books, perspective, sky, earth,
ground, dirt, dearly departed, customs, energy, sadness, fear,
spirit, poetry, God, dog, cat, sister, brother, daughter, family,
you, poems, nights, thoughts, secrets, habits, lines, grievances,
breaks, memories, nightmares, mornings, faith, desire, sex,
funerals, metaphors, histories, names, tongues, syntax, coffee,
smoke, eyes, addiction, witness, paper, fingers, skin, *you, your,*
you're here, there, the sky, the rain, the past, sleep, rest, live, stop,
go, breathe

Sharif S. Elmusa

Within a year of his birth in Palestine in 1947, Sharif S. Elmusa and his family were made refugees. He grew up in a refugee camp in Jericho. He eventually left to attend Cairo University, then earned a master's degree from Northeastern University in Boston and in 1987 received a Ph.D. from the Massachusetts Institute of Technology. His poems have appeared in numerous journals and anthologies, including *Poetry East,* the *Christian Science Monitor,* and *Banipal.* His poetry has been described as "meditative and melancholic," probing the "untrodden areas of sadness." Through poems that are at once strongly personal and engaged in the communal, "Elmusa succeeds in subverting the definition of freedom maintained by the West in relation to Palestine." In addition to poetry, he has produced scholarly writings and translations and, with Gregory Orfalea, coedited *Grape Leaves: A Century of Arab-American Poetry.* He is currently a professor of political science at the American University of Cairo.

Flawed Landscape

And it came to pass,
we lost the war
and became a nation of refugees.
It is always the beginning.
Fueled by fear, my father gathered
the clan, lugged me in his arms,
and headed, on his peasant feet,
across plain and impassable mountains,
without a compass, headed east.

We set down in a desert
without the sinuous sands
of the movies, in a camp,

by the gateless Jericho.
In that flawed landscape,
under the shadow of the dark rocks
of the Mount of Temptation
the world was kind to us.
The United Nations, our godfather,
doled out flour and rice
and cheddar, "yellow," cheese—
sharp beyond our palates.

My father remembered
his twelve olive trees
every day for ten years.
He remembered the peasant saying
to the olive tree Had she felt for his toil,
she'd yield not olives, but tears,
and the tree answering:
"Tears you have enough; I give you oil
to light your lamps, to nourish, and to heal."
Then one day he let go. Let go.
My father was no Ulysses.
He found a new land
and stayed away on the farm,
eking out some rough happiness.

My mother stayed home,
shepherded a pack of twelve,
cleaned and yelled and, for punishment,
summoned father's shadow.
She stuffed our thin bones with sentiments,
as if to make us immobile.

Her past was insatiable:
The new house they had just built,
with windows on four sides,
windows tall and arched
to let in the ample light,
to spread out the prayers;
how my father rushed to ask for her hand
the day after she had kept him in line
at the water well;
how they found the body of her brother
soaked in sweet-scented blood,
in the police station, after he was killed
by the discriminate bullets of the British soldiers.

No statues were built in the camp;
the dead would have been ashamed.
The living dreamed—the dreams of the wounded.
In their houses the radio was the hearth,
and news the oracle.

With New Englanders

I miss my Boston dentist.
The first time I met him,
before injecting the Novocain
into my anxious gums,
he paused
and asked where I was from.
From Palestine, I answered.
"How is the weather in Palestine?"
he wanted to know.

The weather there is temperate,
soil terra rosa.
The shepherds on the hills
have all but disappeared.
Winter sends modest rains,
animates the hardened earth:
red poppies swaying in the breeze,
little spokesmen of beauty;
cotton flowers, purple,
on erect stems, the sting of their thorns
final, like the rebellious gestures of Jesus.
Summer's sun is reliable, vertical.
The old man would be dejected
without cartloads of watermelons.
No blunt pleasures.
Season blends into season
in good faith.

With New Englanders
you muffle the sandstorms.

Roots

Home is where people can read your name
correctly on the tombstone

                                                    Attila József

At birth my parents called me
Sharif Said Hussein Elmusa
and on and on—a caravan of names
lagging behind
as if to rein me in from straying
on the crooked routes.

But one night, on a high balcony
under full, urban moon,
a mountain woman
from the Rockies held me
in the clear pond of her eyes,
as if I was the first Adam.
And I followed love.

Uncle Sam,
casual and efficient,
inventor of the T-shirt,
that simplifier of the race,
found my name baroque,
bulging with self-importance,
yanked out grandfather
and downsized father
even before old age
to an initial, S.
Then the editors finished the job,
excised the atavistic S.
and left me to dream—

like someone who had lost his paradise—
I walked in stealth
in the city streets, with bare feet,
and only my underwear on.

See, my incurable yen
to keep going or coming
to Damascus and Rabat
Cairo and Amman
is not just turning the other cheek.
There, the security men at the border
keep their rugged names and moustaches,
scrutinize my left-to-right passport,
and poke fun at me for going back home
to Washington. They never fail
to ask about my father's name;
and I savor enunciating it:
Said Hussein.

More satisfying, still,
are the gatekeepers of Israel.
How they relish information.
They don't let go
until they have dug up,
among other things,
the names of my birth place,
the village their fathers
and grandfathers had taken
and re-configured, dwellings and name;
until they had dug up my known lineage
right down to the clan.

    Call me
        Sharif.

Should You Wish to Stay

We don't have bicycle lanes marked
by wine-red paint. Every day we stage
the grand opera, How things don't work.
Perfection is as rare as rainfall or smallpox.

But we always keep humor,
that diligent rescue worker, on call.
The tourist, taken aback,
knotting his eyebrows, summons the waiter:
A mouse just crawled by the table.
Waiter: Oh, I'm sorry. Was it big or small?
Tourist: I guess it was small.
Waiter: Good. Then it wasn't one of ours. Ours are big.
Dinner resumes.
History moves on, a rickety cab,
zigzagging, chaotically, like ourselves,
on the banks of the subdued river,
without night lights,
the door opens only from the outside.

Still, don't let the reformer's fire burn
in your chest. The same man
who hogs your turn in the queue
with a glad heart walks you five blocks away
to the store you are looking for.
If the whistle of the rusty freight train
grates your ear, take it for what it is:
a politician's rhetoric
independent of the freight.
Listen and watch the mint leaf

float in the dark-red tea,
a village in a glass; watch our feet walk,
gingerly, the way the flesh doubts.
You may prize hard work, but only in rest
and repose can you sort out the tangled heart,
can you find happiness.

We are still made from the tears of Ra.
The spirits of unseen deities,
borne by the wind blowing from the desert,
coach us while we sleep in the demanding art
of dying well. But you are welcome to discover yourself.
The lavish, matter-of-fact sunlight
will save you further guidance.

Sun Lines

In his last days in Italy
Nietzsche wrote to a friend:
"When you're lonely
you become
friends with the sun."

Is the field of sunflowers a lonely crowd?

Why does the snake go into long sleep
when the sun orbits far away?

Whom does a lonely man in a dark
Siberian winter take for a friend?

Was the architect who dreamed the obelisk
lying, lonely, under a palm tree?

Mohammad received his first word
from Gabriel in the cave.

The loneliness of Jesus led him to Golgotha.

I don't know much about the Buddha,
but his visage looks bathed in sunrays.

How far can we trust the thoughts
of lonely men?

The lovers opt for the moon light.

Hedy Habra

Of Lebanese descent, Hedy Habra was born in Heliopolis, Egypt. She stud-ied at the Faculté Française de Médecine et de Pharmacie of Beirut and, after living for several years in Brussels, moved to the United States, where she earned degrees in English and a Ph.D. in Spanish literature from Western Michigan University. In addition to poetry, she has written critical studies on Spanish and Latin American authors and translated the work of Dominican poets into English. Habra's first poetry book is *Tea in Heliopolis*.

Even the Sun Has Its Dark Side

but does it really matter,
    unless
we could enter that hidden space,
    the way grains of sand
        would suddenly rise

in an hourglass,
    reshape themselves,
    regain their initial place.
I wonder what is lost behind a picture,
    rippled in its negative
as I often try to read between the lines,
    sense clenched teeth,
        or grasp an unspoken word.

When I set to bridge these gaps,
my blood warms up in tides,
    revealing a tightness in the chest
        as if memories,
    pressed in a tin can

kept near one's heart,
could sweep away the gray outside.

We lost everything when we fled,
except for an album
        full of my childhood pictures in Egypt
        and my children born in Beirut.
"You're so lucky," everyone said,
     our family unharmed,
          not one of their fingers
          was worth the whole world
left behind.
     Our beds were made in places where
     the sun teased us, hiding most of the
     time, forcing us to master the local motto
        . . . make sunshine inside . . .
Christmases followed one another
     offering versions of our lives,
          each fragmented image
evoking a new face,
     a recipe . . . an absence . . .

Whenever I sort them out,
     I see myself floating in a fluid
          lining edges
in search of a referent that has vanished,
        leaving only an empty shell,
     crumpled, discolored like fallen leaves.

I felt constantly renewed,
     peeled off like an onion,
         shedding layer after layer

until what was left
was so tender,
　　　une primeur à déguster,
　　　　　yet so vulnerable,
then wings grew
overlapping its core
　　　to mend what was undone,
　　　　　like praying hands
　　　in different tongues
while children rebelled against
　　　whatever came from a distant land,
the repotted bulb spread roots
　　　in the New World's moist soil
　　　　　until it looked whole again.
And year after year we learned
to sit in front of the camera,
　　　　gather a succession
　　　　　　of perfect moments
till I lost track of what lies under these smiles.

How could I ever part
with my old black and white photographs,
　　　taken when I was a little girl
　　　　　and no one forced me to smile,
　　　yet I knew how loved I was . . . pictures
of my parents proudly seated in a mock airplane
about to take off . . .
　　　　. . . my mother's delicate lace net
　　　　coming down her *toque,*
　　　　half-covering her eyes, head
　　　　slanted in an enigmatic look
　　　　　a la Garbo . . . my father in

black tie and white scarf, a tall
hat in his hand.

I see you posing with us, mother.
    Your age, the same as mine,
playing a role,
    a proud, perfect mother. Yet, I never
saw you happy, I mean really . . . Nothing like
our pictures, the four of us radiant,
    year after year.
        I got used to smiling, you know, thought
it made me look younger,
        helped hide the wrinkles.
After capturing the sun inside me,
    now the peer pressure . . .
        . . . the need for American beauty.

Milkweed

Only at dusk is one swept by the deep
sweet scent of milkweed,
a turbulence
in the evening's crisp air. Scepters,
edging the road in triple rows,
crowned by pink,
minute star-like flowers
linked by invisible rays.

I pull the thick stem, an ancestral
gesture,
freeing hairy filaments
from rain-soaked earth, to bury
in the creek's
moist soil.
Rubbing my sticky fingers, I wonder
what powers lie
in the white bleeding
of broken leaves, the stigmata of purple
veins, cures lost
with old shamans,
before this land was named Michigan.

And I think of Lebanon, the green figs
we grew in the mountains
of Baabdat,
figs picked, children climbing forbidden
fences. At the bottom of each fig,
a white tear
covered the circular scar,

a tear, beading from invisible pores,
sheathing our skin
with transparent gloves.

I hear my mother's voice, an echo
of ancient wisdom,
purification rites:
"Never rub your eyes before washing
or you'll go blind!" Would milkweed
sap heal
sightless eyes, unaware
of star-like flowers
offering their last silk-winged seed?

A swarm of bees milks intangible beads;
I inhale the dizzying
scent, anchoring
myself in increasing darkness. A spark
reveals hidden berries,
the whiteness
of a Daisy, Queen Anne's lace,
fireflies,
springing from nowhere,
greener in a darkened back alley
between three black

trunks, rising motes of flame
in the cool liminal hour,
vision inside vision,
inside me, at the verge of the night,
the wild dance
of heated elytra
everywhere around grass and wildflower,

attentive only to that mysterious,
incoherent language,
emerging from folds
of bark, creased blades of grass,
moisture trapped
in lichen, in humus,
underneath blackened oak leaves.

Tea at *Chez Paul's*

We ate Schtengels at *Chez Paul's*,
twisted bread sprinkled with coarse salt
    clinging to our lips.
We could see the sea enfolding us
through the tall bay windows
of the semi-circular Swiss teahouse.
You described a Phoenician Tale
just for me,
how the mountain slopes
reddened each spring
    with Adonis' blood,
how this delicate flower,
truly and duly Lebanese
has come to be called a red poppy, an anemone,
with all its melodious variations,
    alkhushkhash,
        un amapola,
            un coquelicot,
                ed anche un papavero . . .

We walked through a field scattered
with red poppies bright as when Ishtar
sprinkled nectar
on her beloved's blood.
    Time seemed elastic then,
        space infinite.
I wished to bring home a handful of scarlet light,
to keep the softness of its wrinkled petals
alive a while longer.

The moment I cut Adonis' flower,
hanging like a broken limb, its corolla fell over my hand,
head too heavy with dreams.
     No wonder blossoms tremble
          on their fragile stem.

Sometimes love is only real when not uprooted.
     Isn't there a geography of every emotion?
not a precious, intricate *Carte du Tendre*,
     but a trail of forgotten footsteps mapping
every heartbeat, every motion?
       A stairwell, a car, a booth, a parking lot,
     a streetlight, a gateway,
an old-fashioned réverbère,
     a Bus Stop or maybe a tree, a tree stump,
a moss-covered path, a pond,
     a small creek, a flat stone,
       a hill, a porch or even a wooden bench?

Take the poppy, for instance. It will only breathe
and give joy at its birthplace.
     I can still feel the small flower melting
into liquid silk in my palm.
     I held the red petals to my cheek
like a morning kiss while you kept telling how Ishtar
     or as some may say Astarté, often mistaken for Isis,
       was truly her Phoenician incarnation,
before she was ever called Aphrodite or Venus.
     I remember how you talked and talked
until we both stepped into Ishtar's temple.

Marian Haddad

Marian Haddad's poems possess a "richness of language and cultural identity" and insist on the "connective instead of divisive" aspects of difference. No doubt, her background informs these traits. Born in El Paso, Texas, to Syrian immigrants, she was the only one of ten siblings to be born in the United States and, in her childhood, spent a good deal of time on the Mexican side of the border. At home she spoke English, Arabic, and Spanish. She is the author of a chapbook, *Saturn Falling Down*, and a full-length collection, *Somewhere between Mexico and a River Called Home*. She graduated from the University of Texas at El Paso, earned an M.F.A. from San Diego State University, received a fellowship from the National Endowment for the Humanities to study philosophy at the University of Notre Dame, and studied the prose poem at Emerson College. She lives in San Antonio.

She Is Not the House of This Black Wing

One of us is dying. Lying in a bed in a hospital suite. Tubes sprawling out of her like roots of a tree deep under the earth. A long plastic cord in her right nostril pumps bile into a large plastic cup attached to the wall above her bed.

• • •

She is resting now. Pink bedspread heaves slowly with each breath. Her coloring is ripe. Her skin is soft as light brown sugar. The mouth cups open, letting air into her lungs. Air. Important. Her legs outlined underneath the sheets, thinner even now.

She winces as she moves. A quick, sharp beep resounds as she presses her pain button. Demerol drips down her IV, numbs the surgical carvings sketched in her skin.

• • •

Flowers line the walls. Roses the color of parchment, the color of membrane, and one sticking up, the color of fire. Fragrant bushes of tiger lilies, orchids metastasizing, azaleas mutating, and a lump of purple peonies like bruises unfolded. Glads rising up out of this night.

What tempests are blowing through the countries in her brain? I know we are numb, and when we are not, we are shaking.

Malfunctioning FLOWTRON

I would say he likes the cadence
of the high pitched beep—he is

sleeping better now—quiet
makes us think—our minds

crank every few minutes, eyes
open, the mouth atwitter

and sleep has slipped. Awake
and thirsty from the Morphine,

he smacks his lips, rolls
his tongue inside, *Agua,*

he says, though he is
not Mexican. *Agua,*

a language he has learned
in America, and he, Arabic.

Three languages roll deftly
on this dry tongue,

awaiting a swab
of water, he sucks it

like the nipple of a mother;
hoping to wash clean

all that is not. And here,
the beep, started and sounding

in its metronomic mode. Now,
he lies snoring, mouth open

wide, the welcome music
of the living.

Resurrection

Ascension of bone against bone.
There is something that clatters
like fangs strung together on twine
about my neck. Black sky vapors.
My grandfather's five moons rise
above me. His wife stands clouding
the door of night, blesses me with her once-
fleshy palm, lays it like ivory twigs
upon my head. A holy garment. The chalice
and the cup. She bids me to find blue,
points to the field of night flowers, white
and heavy with damp. I kneel in-between rows
of petals and stems, scent seeping. Camphor
of night. She bids me to immerse myself in water,
past the patch of trees. She prays I will bear
children, that they will swim like truth
around my sphere. She names me
Saturn, and I bow to her presence
in silence, her bones clattering a prayer,
near and around me.

I have no history here

nothing but a year
and a few months of turning

I have made a home
in a land I never knew

where people seem distant
and unhearing

yet in-between the crowds
a few comrades

I am starting to write myself
down   inscribe myself

somewhere near
these waters

are we not all welcome
in this salty land by sea

out my window   the sun
no longer   the night   nearing

a few lights   yellow
and white between hills

something quiet
about this place

this is no desert
the air here is damp

water seems present
where water is not

my southwest skin
has scaled off

dropping quietly
into this grass

Suheir Hammad

Suheir Hammad has been described as "a new voice with an authentic blend of language that's her own," and her poems have received wide acclaim. She is the recipient of an Audre Lorde Writing Award, an Emerging Artist Award, and a Tony Award as an original cast member and writer for Russell Simmons Presents Def Poetry Jam on Broadway. Hammad's poetry often engages "culture, conflict, and consciousness," which is not surprising given her background. Born in a Palestinian refugee camp in Jordan, she immigrated to Brooklyn at the age of five. She travels abroad frequently, as a poet and activist, and has read her work at universities, on the BBC, on NPR, and in prisons. Her books include the poetry collections *Born Palestinian, Born Black* and *ZaatarDiva* and a memoir, *Drops of This Story.*

Silence

I wonder what he
heard as he ran
wonder what he
thought as the
    american bullets
flew from
    israeli hands
through
    god's air
to murder another
one of freedom's sons

he didn't look back

did he hear the loud strong
voices of our women
voices so clear

songs so sad   so beautiful
strained   drained
by years of crying
(singing) *Ishad ya, dlam alena wa d Beirut*
            Ishad il hdrb il shabiyeh
            (Bear witness world to us and to Beirut
            Bear witness to the War of Liberation)

did he hear the
angels who'd proclaimed the birth
of jesus in that same land
angels singing songs of
heaven   angels who arose from
the earth after dying
too young in the
name of palestine

ran so fast
as his brown feet
touched loved   touched loved
the brown earth
did he hear his
mama singing him
to sleep

he had lived with his eyes

seen so much
palestine occupied   freedom denied   my people's genocide
seen with his eyes
felt with his heart
struggle of life under
army boots

palestine alive

(singing) *Wa men ma shaf bil ghorban ya Beirut*

Aman ayoon Amreeciya

(And those who don't see through the sieve

Are blinded by American eyes)

not been blinded by

american eyes

saw it all and he

knew what did he

hear as he ran

so used to running

we are   it seems

we palestinians are always running

where do we go

never looking back

Ishad ya alam alene wa a Beirut

(Bear witness world to us and to Beirut)

they warned him to stop

called out in the name of

democracy and violence

called out in the tongue

of the ancients to

halt his running

they fired their

american made bullets

did he hear them

from israeli hands

through god's air

into palestine's son
(singing)

they labeled it
an accidental
but necessary death
when discovered this
son of palestine
had been born
deaf
(singing)
Wa men shaf bil ghorban ya Beirut Aman ayoon Amreeciya

exotic

don't wanna be your exotic

     some delicate   fragile   colorful bird

     imprisoned   caged

     in a land foreign to the stretch of her wings

don't wanna be your exotic

     women everywhere are just like me

     some taller   darker   nicer than me

     but like me but just the same

     women everywhere carry my nose on their faces

     my name on their spirits

don't wanna

     don't seduce yourself with

     my otherness   my hair

     wasn't put on top of my head to entice

     you into some mysterious black voodoo

     the beat of my lashes against each other

     ain't some dark desert beat

     it's just a blink

     get over it

don't wanna be your exotic

     your lovin of my beauty ain't more than

     funky fornication   plain pink perversion

     in fact   nasty necrophilia

     cause my beauty is dead to you

     I am dead to you

not your

     harem girl   geisha doll   banana picker

     pom pom girl pum pum shorts   coffee maker

town whore   belly dancer   private dancer
la malinche   venus hottentot   laundry girl
your immaculate vessel emasculating princess

don't wanna be
       your erotic
not your exotic

First Writing Since

1. there have been no words.
i have not written one word.
no poetry in the ashes south of canal street.
no prose in the refrigerated trucks driving debris and dna.
not one word.

today is a week, and seven is of heavens, gods, science.
evident out my kitchen window is an abstract reality.
sky where once was steel.
smoke where once was flesh.

fire in the city air and i feared for my sister's life in a way never
before. and then, and now, i fear for the rest of us.

first, please god, let it be a mistake, the pilot's heart failed,
the plane's engine died.
then please god, let it be a nightmare, wake me now.
please god, after the second plane, please, don't let it be anyone
who looks like my brothers.

i do not know how bad a life has to break in order to kill.
i have never been so hungry that i willed hunger
i have never been so angry as to want to control a gun over a pen.

not really.
even as a woman, as a palestinian, as a broken human being.
never this broken.

more than ever, i believe there is no difference.
the most privileged nation, most americans do not know the difference
between indians, afghanis, syrians, muslims, sikhs, hindus.
more than ever, there is no difference.

2. thank you korea for kimchi and bibim bob, and corn tea and the
genteel smiles of the wait staff at wonjo smiles never revealing
the heat of the food or how tired they must be working long midtown
shifts. thank you korea, for the belly craving that brought me into
the city late the night before and diverted my daily train ride into
the world trade center.

there are plenty of thank yous in ny right now.
thank you for my lazy procrastinating late ass.
thank you to the germs that had me call in sick.
thank you, my attitude, you had me fired the week before.
thank you for the train that never came,
the rude nyer who stole my cab going downtown.
thank you for the sense my mama gave me to run.
thank you for my legs, my eyes, my life.

3. the dead are called lost and their families hold up shaky
printouts in front of us through screens smoked up.

we are looking for iris, mother of three. please call with any
information. we are searching for priti, last seen on the 103rd
floor. she was talking to her husband on the phone and the line
went. please help us find george, also known as adel. his family is
waiting for him with his favorite meal. i am looking for my son, who

was delivering coffee. i am looking for my sister girl,
she started her job on monday.

i am looking for peace. i am looking for mercy. i am looking for
evidence of compassion. any evidence of life. i am looking for life.

4. ricardo on the radio said in his accent thick as yuca, "i will
feel so much better when the first bombs drop over there. and my
friends feel the same way."

on my block, a woman was crying in a car parked and stranded in hurt.
i offered comfort, extended a hand she did not see before she said,
"we're gonna burn them so bad, i swear, so bad." my hand went to my
head and my head went to the numbers within it of the dead iraqi
children, the dead in nicaragua. the dead in rwanda who had to vie
with fake sport wrestling for america's attention.

yet when people sent emails saying, this was bound to happen, let's
not forget u.s. transgressions, for half a second i felt resentful.
hold up with that, cause i live here, these are my friends and fam,
and it could have been me in those buildings, and we're not bad
people, do not support america's bullying.
can i just have a half second to feel bad?

if i can find through this exhaust people who were left behind to
mourn and to resist mass murder, i might be alright.

thank you to the woman who saw me brinking my cool and blinking back
tears. she opened her arms before she asked "do you want a hug?" a
big white woman, and her embrace was the kind only people with the
warmth of flesh can offer. i wasn't about to say no to any comfort.
"my brother's in the navy," i said. "and we're arabs."
"wow, you got double trouble." word.

5. one more person ask me if i knew the hijackers.
one more motherfucker ask me what navy my brother is in.
one more person assume no arabs or muslims were killed.
one more person assume they know me, or that i represent a people.
or that a people represent an evil.
or that evil is as simple as a flag and words on a page.

we did not vilify all white men when mcveigh bombed oklahoma.
america did not give out his family's addresses or where he went to
church. or blame the bible or pat robertson.

and when the networks air footage of palestinians dancing in the
street, there is no apology for hungry children who are bribed with
sweets that turn their teeth brown. that correspondents edit images.
that archives are there to facilitate lazy and inaccurate
journalism.

and when we talk about holy books and hooded men and death,
why do we never mention the kkk?

if there are any people on earth who understand
how new york is feeling right now,
they are in the west bank and the gaza strip.

6. today it is ten days. last night bush waged war on a man once
openly funded by the cia. i do not know who is responsible. read too many
books, know too many people to believe what i am told. i don't give a fuck
about bin laden. his vision of the world does not include me or those
i love. and petitions have been going around for years trying to get
the u.s. sponsored taliban out of power. shit is complicated,
and i don't know what to think.

but i know for sure who will pay.

in the world, it will be women, mostly colored and poor. women will
have to bury children, and support themselves through grief.
"either you are with us, or with the terrorists"
meaning keep your people under control and your resistance censored.
meaning we got the loot
and the nukes.

in america, it will be those amongst us who refuse blanket attacks
on the shivering. those of us who work toward social justice, in
support of civil liberties, in opposition to hateful foreign policies.

i have never felt less american and more new yorker—particularly
brooklyn, than these past days. the stars and stripes on all these
cars and apartment windows represent the dead as citizens first
not family members, not lovers.

i feel like my skin is real thin, and that my eyes are only going to
get darker. the future holds little light.

my baby brother is a man now, and on alert, and praying five times a
day that the orders he will take in a few days time are righteous and
will not weigh his soul down from the afterlife he deserves.

both my brothers—my heart stops when i try to pray—not a beat to
disturb my fear. one a rock god, the other a sergeant, and both
palestinian, practicing muslim, gentle men. both born in brooklyn
and their faces are of the archetypal arab man, all eyelashes and
nose and beautiful color and stubborn hair.

what will their lives be like now?

over there is over here.

7. all day, across the river, the smell of burning rubber and limbs
floats through. the sirens have stopped now.
the advertisers are back on the air.
the rescue workers are traumatized.
the skyline is brought back to human size.
no longer taunting the gods with its height.

i have not cried at all while writing this. i cried when i saw those
buildings collapse on themselves like a broken heart. i have never
owned pain that needs to spread like that. and i cry daily that my
brothers return to our mother safe and whole.

there is no poetry in this. there are causes and effects. there are
symbols and ideologies. mad conspiracy here, and information we will
never know. there is death here, and there are promises of more.

there is life here. anyone reading this is breathing, maybe hurting,
but breathing for sure. and if there is any light to come, it will
shine from the eyes of those who look for peace and justice after the
rubble and rhetoric are cleared and the phoenix has risen.

affirm life.
affirm life.
we got to carry each other now.
you are either with life, or against it.
affirm life.

mike check

one two one two can you
hear me mic check one two

mike checked
my bags at the air
port in a random
routine check

i understand mike i do
you too were altered
that day and most days
most folks operate on
fear often hate this
is mic check your
job and i am
always random

i understand it was
folks who looked smelled
maybe prayed like me

can you hear me mike
ruddy blonde buzz
cut with corn flower
eyes and a cross
round your neck

mike check
folks who looked like
you stank so bad the

indians smelled them
mic check before they landed

they murdered one two
one two as they prayed
spread small pox as alms

mic check yes i
packed my own
bags can you hear
me no they have not
been out of my possession

thanks mike you
have a good day too one
two check mike
check mike

a-yo mike
whose gonna
check you?

Sam Hamod

Sam Hamod's poems arise from "a full, generous heart" and a sensibility "keenly attuned to subtleties of feelings and perceptions." Hamod is the author of more than ten poetry books, most recently *Dying with the Wrong Name: New and Selected Poems: 1966–1980*, *The Arab Poems*, *The Muslim Poems*, and *Just Love Poems for You*. Hamod has taught at the Iowa Writers' Workshop, Princeton, and the University of Michigan and has served as a State Department advisor on Islamic and Middle Eastern Affairs. One of the first Arab American poets to have a poetry book published, Hamod has received numerous awards, among them grants from the National Endowment for the Arts and the National Endowment for the Humanities and an Ethnic Heritage Award.

Dying with the Wrong Name

These men died with the wrong names,
Na'aim Jazeeney, from the beautiful valley
Of Jezzine,
died as Nephew Sam.
Eh'sine Hussin died without relatives and
Because they cut away his last name
At Ellis Island, there was no way to trace him
Back even to Lebanon
And Ima' Brahim had no other name than
Mother of Brahim
Even my own father lost his, went from
Hussein Hamode Subh' to Sam Hamod.
There is something lost in the blood,
Something lost down to the bone
In these small changes
a man

In a dark blue uniform
at Ellis Island says, with
Tiredness and authority,
"You only need two
Names in America," and suddenly
cleanly as air
You've lost
Your name.
At first, it's hardly
Even noticeable—it's easier, you can move about
As an American—but looking back
The loss of your name
Cuts away some other part,
Something unspeakable
is lost.

II

And I know, these were not small men,
Each was severe, though part
Comic,
as we will all be remembered—but Nephew
Sam ran a cigar store in Michigan City,
in the back room
his poker game with chips and bills often past
$30,000; when I was a little boy,
I saw, in his middle years, Eh'sine Hussin
lift the rear end of a '39 Ford
so they could
change a tire
and my father who threw men to the ground
twice his size went
from Lebanon to the packing houses in Sioux Falls and

Sioux City to the steel mills in Gary—
we went from living in a single room
where the windows rattled every morning
when the trains rumbled by on the E J & E,
B & O and the Pennys,
in that rented South Shore Hotel
he and my mother ran as a boarding house,
in each drop of movement from
5 A.M. cooking food for the gandy dancers and millworkers
to nights working in the Broadway Tavern
at 17th & Broadway,
selling scotch and bootleg Canadian Whiskey while
B. B. King, T. Bone Walker hustled blues, each
dollar another day
mixing names and money, money and
music with Vivian Carter starting VJ records
in the corner store behind
his bar,   ah—
these were men,
men who opened the world with a gesture of their hand,
a nod and things moved, houses were built
for each new relative, apartment buildings were bought and sold,
cars given as wedding presents, mayors and congressmen
were bought and sold, made and broken—
but promises always kept.
These men
live now on the edge of myth—each one under a
stone a stone carved in English, the Arabic of
Hussein Hamode Subh', Na'aim Jazeeney, Eh'sine Hussin
lost
each one sealed away
with the wrong

name
except in this poem
but a poem goes out
to so few
but we do what we can
and we trust in what we must

III

Eh'sine Hussin is still sitting in that old
Chair, upholstered in brushed maroon wool, he
Sits with his back to the window
Inward, at an angle, the antique crystal lamp rests
On the ornate mahogany table—Ima' Brahim.
Full-veined and old, barely managing to
Walk, a
Short osman of a woman no more than 4foot7 or so, but
Obviously before her first child,
The cameo shape of her face was more
Delicate—and
You know the smell of this room, fresh lamb and fried
Onions, pungent garlic on the salad, tartness of lemon
Twists into the air, and an ease settles in
toward evening as we walk in, then
All the silence splits into hellos and hugs,
"Ahlan, Ahlan Wa Sahlan, Assalamu Alaikum . . ."
suddenly the world comes together
In this small antique room—
Somehow, I understood
what this old couple meant
to my father, words
he never spoke,
but were there in his eyes

in the tears he sometimes
lost when they'd passed on,
his own father died before my father came
to America in 1914, his mother still in Lebanon,
unseen for decades.

My father is 39 or 40 now, I
Am 4 or 5, we are constantly carrying groceries
To this old house at 301 Monroe Street, with Eh'sine
Hussin and Ima' Brahim always saying, "La, no—we don't need
Anything,"
but they are forced
to take the tomatoes, lettuce, cucumbers, lemons, apples
and the fresh lamb—but
Only after we've eaten some fati'ya and coffee "eat some
fruit, ya habeebee, eat some more, come on,"
then talk, talk, talk (I'm usually impatient to go—
I'm sleepy and stuffed)
finally, after long hugs
and long sentences in Arabic I can't understand,
my father and I pull away
from the outstretched arms,
then we climb back into the old Chrysler
and we have a long,
a kind of lonely ride back home.
You want to leave
but also yearn
to stay, but each time you leave,
you feel a deep sense of loneliness, you
want to be in both places at the same time,
but as a child—you don't know what it is.
As for my father, he was a man I came to know

As secretive, generous, a man
Alone—
and now I understand,
this old couple
Was a part of that other reality,
where his name,
in that other language than English,
that was more than just Arabic,
it was that deep spirit, Hussein,
Hussein Hamode Subh', Eh'sine Hussin, Ima' Brahim,
Assalamu Alaikum,
all of these sounds,
these words,
were part of his name,
this was that other part of Lebanon he carried within him, that
Home, these same good people,
that same good food
of these rich aromas,
It had to be in these moments
That these things were not lost,
but were alive and living
in this room,
in this house,
in these people
in this moment

    V

And now, the South Shore Hotel at 3rd and Jefferson
Has vanished with
Urban renewal,
As has the old stucco house at 3rd and Monroe, and
I don't remember where Eh'sine Hussin is

Buried, and my mother and father rest
Next to my grandfather, the Hajj Abbass Habhab,
in a grassy cemetery in Cedar Rapids, Iowa—far
From the action of Gary and Chicago, far from the
Heady days of building businesses, building families,
building Mosques
and converting Elijah Muhammad's people to
Islam—it is far from the evenings at 11th and Wallace
to the Mosque El Ameen,
When Jamil Diab would bring busloads
of Black Muslims
From Chicago, and the chanting
of prayers would go on
Into the nights, it is far from
The afternoons when we as children
Would study Arabic and Islam at the mosques
In Michigan City and Cedar Rapids,
When we'd play football for an hour then
Study those funny looking lines that our fathers loved,
an alphabet we didn't believe in, not
knowing why we were supposed to learn Arabic, or
Why we were there—to us,
that language belonged to that other
Place, that place we'd never seen, but whose presence
Filled our homes, filled our
Lives—so when we were in the house, we were in old Lebanon,
Pre-French Lebanon, and when we hit the street,
we were in Gary,
In Cedar Rapids, in Michigan City, in Toledo and Detroit where
Our fathers wielded power and money
With ease, though they could not write the language, they
Knew how to use it, and we understood

From them, that this was how
It was done— so we did,
Each of us did those things we
Learned, some stayed in the bars and the restaurants
and others of us ventured forth
And some even wrote poems—but it all washes
Like Tom Sawyer's whitewash—we remember
The best, forget most of the rest—that is the
Best way, but now, we wish
we could remember even more—
and those sounds of Mahmoud Hoballah,
Sheikh Muhammad Jawad Chirri and Sheikh Kamal
Avdich remain in our ears, as our fathers keep telling us,
"Learn, ya ibn abouk-learn . . ."
and so we learned, and to this day
we remember
we remember
and our hearts break with a deep sorrow
because we understood so little

VI

Now our children, strangely enough
Have learned the language, learned the
Arabic better than we
It's almost as if they
Heard our fathers, or maybe it's that
Our fathers' spirits were so strong
That they refused to stay
In their graves, but came back
And insisted that our children, our boys,
my son, David, my cousin's son, Tarik, and the rest,
learned Arabic,

learned how to do their
Prayers, that they held strong
In their sway to keep their
Voices alive, to keep their strength
Alive, whether it be William, Yehya
Aossey in Iowa, or Sam Hussein
Hamod Subh' in Gary, Indiana—they
Moved our children
In their direction—they gave up
On us, we were too much like
Them, we were
Stubborn, and just as they ventured
Out, lit out on their
Own, so too did we, so we
Went forth in our directions—away
From our fathers' directions
And made our own
Way—but they spoke to our
Children, and those same
aromas, events stay alive—for us, in our
Memories, in them, on the tables
Whether they are in Qatar, Saudi
Arabia, Syria or Lebanon, they know
When it is time to pray, and they carry
An odd heritage—we, and they, we are
The original Arabs, we are the original
Muslims, our heads unbowed, because we
We are lucky that our fathers left Lebanon
Before the French, so we are free, and
We have never tasted
Captivity—so we carry that "old Arab tradition,
of the honorable, strong and just man, that

true sense of Islam as humble before God
only doing what is right, with love and respect
for all men and all religions," that our fathers fed into
Our minds, into our
Hearts, that sense of humility and pride that lack of
Fear, that sense that you can do what you want,
Without wasting time on
Fear—and so did learn, as I told one man,
when I was Director of The Islamic Center
in Washington, DC,
When he said to me, "You aren't a real Arab
Or a real Muslim"—I answered,
"We are the real thing—no one ever conquered
us, no one ever bought us, and we come to our religion
and culture not by governance but by choice"
and so we are here today,
carrying within us those same sounds, those same
smells remembered from our
childhood, the onions and garlic, the
fresh tomatoes and lemons, the parsley,
the smoke of fresh lamb, the deep voice of
the Imam chanting the Qur'an
and the calligraphies and Arabic poems
in a script hard for us to translate, but
that we understand in our hearts.

Lara Hamza

Lara Hamza was born in Beirut and by the age of six had lived in Lebanon, Libya, Bahrain, and the United States. Her family shuffled between Florida and Michigan, eventually settling in the latter, where she now lives and teaches. She was educated at the University of Michigan and Ohio State University. Her poems possess "a uniquely 'liminal' voice—at once paradigmatic and 'fabulistic'—in effect, seizing the prose poem as her own emblematic lyric form." Hamza cites as among her influences Charles Baudelaire, Charles Bukowski, Albert Camus, and Russell Edson. She prefers the prose form, which releases language from the restrictions of line and reveals the darker, sometimes humorous aspects of her subjects.

Advice for Marriage

You can't walk into a vegetable store and come out with gold. I dreamed of gold once, and ended up with a potato—*Why?* I was destined for a potato. *You?* You're different. You will have gold—*Why?* Because *you* can! *You* really can! Let us go to the jewelers, you and I. Here, use your teaspoon; melt your honey in your drink.

My Mother Wore Miniskirts

Now she's a Hajji. Made her pilgrimage this year. Brought back prayer rugs, told me to choose. I chose red with shiny gold thread. Red seemed least holy, red seemed to fit. *Please try,* she begs me, *please try to pray.* I can count on a pamphlet every four years: high school, college, graduate school. I open and read them, look closely at the sketches. This is how you wash: elbows, arms, forehead, feet. This is how you kneel and rise, and this is what you say: *Bis-millah Al-Rahman Al-Rahime.* In the name of God, the Beneficent, the Merciful. How pretty her legs were in old black and white: slender, long, and free. *But that was the devil,* she tells me, *the devil I didn't know.* I keep my rug rolled tightly beneath my bed. The beads inside its pocket worry me to sleep: *Why don't you try? Why won't you try?* The smooth stone from Mecca waits for a kiss.

Behind Locked Doors, Part I

Please come out and greet the guests. It's rude to stay in your bedroom when we have company. Open up. I want to show you a new dress. Don't you want to see my new dress? Your grandmother called today. I sure miss her. When you're older you'll regret this. You'll regret having me stand behind your door like a beggar, and you'll miss me more than I now miss my mother! Let me in! Why won't you let me in? Please unlock your door! Damn this country! Is this what they teach you here? Is this what they teach you!

Growing Up

The patent leather shoes, with the thin strap and buckle, cut through both ankles, and stained my white tights.

On Eating

We gathered around the dinner table, my three brothers, mother, father, and me. My father cooked steak and potatoes that evening. I knew they didn't expect me to eat because for almost a year, I had stopped. Dad cooked only five pieces of steak. And when I reached for one and put it on my plate no one questioned. I cut it into ten tiny pieces and put a tiny drop of ketchup on each one. The meat was well cooked and tender. I chewed slowly, counting to twenty-five each time. Please, take my piece, my mother said to my father. But he refused. Don't worry, he said. He ate only the potatoes. After chewing the tenth bite, I went to the bathroom, stuck two fingers deep inside my throat, and threw up my meal. This is how I started eating again. It took a while to learn how to keep things inside.

Nathalie Handal

Born to Palestinian parents, Nathalie Handal has lived in Europe, the United States, the Caribbean, Latin America, and the Arab world. She studied English and drama at the University of London, fiction writing at Humber College in Toronto, and poetry at Bennington College and also earned degrees from Simmons College in Boston. Her poems, collected in two books, *The Neverfield* and *The Lives of Rain*, have been translated into over a dozen languages. While displacement, exile, and the struggles of the human condition are common themes in her poems, "the weightiness of her subjects is delightfully at odds with the buoyancy of her cadence." Handal has also edited several anthologies, including *The Poetry of Arab Women*, which received the PEN Oakland/Josephine Miles Award and was an Academy of American Poets bestseller. She has also written, directed, or produced over twelve film and theatrical productions and is currently in residence at the New York Theatre Workshop.

The Warrior

It was Wednesday, I remember. Maybe it was Thursday. I had arrived early, early enough to drink some good wine alone with a man I thought we all should fear and for a second forgot. Then they arrived. Nothing in me had changed, even after the wine, even after I saw a goat and corpse cut open side by side. Some say this place is cursed, every drop of water sinks the earth. Strange the things one thinks about at moments like this—was I a stranger to the lover who saw my curves and scars, kissed them then slept like a deserter? Strange what comes to you in the dream-shadows of God—children you saw once in Nablus or Ramallah, who told you the hour the dates will grow in Palestine. Then they arrived. Announced—she died yesterday, but I heard she died a year ago, later that evening I found out she will die tomorrow. And then I heard him say, *Shut up, there is only one way to fight a war. Become the other.* I cross my legs and take his face apart trying to find a way to remember this moment otherwise.

The Combatant and I

It's been a long time—
where have you been, where are you?
I miss your frowns,
the dark shadow on your oval chin.
I can't breathe at night, can't feel my legs.
Dreamed I stopped seeing.
Are you lost?
Are you returning? Am I returning?
I suppose you would say,
I should be happy that I can still love.

It's been a long time.
Stop looking at me from so far, come to me,
stop following me, come to me,
through these dark alleys,
yellow-green forests, these hills of stone,
rows of olives and lives;
stop walking behind me, come to me,
you make me lose my way and ways . . .
I look out the window and think of
the shadows behind your shadows
we both don't recognize,
think that between us,
sleeps the words we had to leave,
think of the movement of hay twirling
on that breezy afternoon we crossed to,
somewhere
we did not expect to be.

The Blue Jacket

Stardust sifts on the shoulders of the blue jacket,
slides down to the end of the sleeves,
finds a place at the tower of my fingers.
I let the asterisks discover the heart of the sheet,
allow the ferries to travel wherever seaweed and lanterns
     call.
I think of the lovesong in the back pocket of a martyr,
the way he continued to walk until the end of the smoke,
remembered the white and yellow pack of cigarettes in his
     shirt pocket.
I knew that I could find color in the curves of branches
but all the color I wanted to see was in the blue jacket.
Subways and war games are afternoon attractions for those who
     survived,
I still live by the blue jacket's rules, its threads healed
     the bruises on the child's feet,
hid the only arak bottle left from the invaders . . .

The blue jacket. I wear it, so I will remember
the day I saw him in dewdrops, the day small ivory thorns found refuge
     in envelopes
       of letters going . . .

from The Neverfield

Decades of riding through skies wearing different
costumes, landing in squares strange to the heart,
feeling like a misplaced light in a dying day, like a
phantom passing through
a village with no one to observe . . .
feeling like a spy, exposing myself
as the tongue speaks everything
with a foreign tone,
continuously spinning around
the wounded moon . . .
feeling abandoned inside the darkest room of myself,
knowing that all the openings are open but none are
mine . . .
later
after stopping in many stations
the mind holds on to one flight—
when
it is not
what language my mouth speaks,
not what landscape my face reflects,
but
the name I carry,
the murmuring of my blood
that
is
my only claim
the only one that really matters . . .

my mind leaves to remember

that place where the grain of my veins
was first harvested,
that place where oranges stopped us
from starving and dust painted itself
on our bare breasts . . .
women
of that place
awoke day after day
polishing the fragmented lamps
and the invisible doorknobs,
sitting under the only almond tree
reciting a prophesy heavier than
the moon's mind . . .
losing their features
in their backyards
but owning a single coat
large enough to warm
the entire village . . .   and I

who let the cities loose
and kept all of the graffiti on the walls,
it was I who took the last poster
of the town before and gave it
to my dead neighbor who fought for it
all his life . . .
it was I, who was I but the reflection
of a people imprisoned in a picture . . .

Samuel Hazo

Poet, novelist, essayist, and playwright Samuel Hazo founded and continues to direct the International Poetry Forum in Pittsburgh, where he is also the McAnulty Distinguished Professor of English Emeritus at Duquesne University. He writes poetry of "immense intelligence, lyricism, and humanity," with "perfect pitch" and "ever-varied grammatical attack." Among his numerous poetry collections are *The Holy Surprise of Right Now; As They Sail; Just Once,* which received the Maurice English Poetry Award; and *A Flight to Elsewhere.* Hazo has also translated the work of several writers, including Denis de Rougemont, Nadia Tueni, and Adonis. A captain in the Marine Corps from 1950 to 1957, Hazo has been awarded nine honorary doctorates. In 1993, he was chosen as the first State Poet of the Commonwealth of Pennsylvania, a post he held for ten years.

Intifada

Singly at first, then doubly,
  then slowly by the tens or twenties,
  then steadily on . . .
      Interviewed
  about the deathcount in Ramallah,
  one sergeant said, "We'll kill
  them all, but we'll never
  forgive them for making us do it."
Later he aimed his Uzi at a boy
  armed with a stone and a slingshot.
One general claimed his soldiers
  fired only rubber-coated bullets.
When asked about the difference
  to the dead, he frowned and shouted,

"Their leaders and parents use
these children as human shields."
Despite the contradicting photographs,
pundits and lobbyists concurred.
After all, who could deny
that boys with all their lives
ahead of them would happily
seek execution, that mothers loved
to see their sons in open
coffins, that choosing a brave
death instead of a lifelong one
was an option for fools?
No one
would claim that occupation
to the occupied resembled daily
suffocation.
No one would add
that suffocation or the fear of it
begot a courage born
of desperation.
No one compared it
to the fate of being locked
in darkness in a stalled elevator
underground.
Like someone buried
upright and alive, anyone
trapped there would stop at nothing.

September 11, 2001

1.

The hawk seems almost napping
    in his glide.
               His arcs are perfect
as geometry.
               His eyes hunger
for something about to panic,
something small and unaware.
Higher by two thousand feet
    an airbus vectors for its port,
its winglights aiming dead
ahead like eyesight.
               The natural
and scheduled worlds keep happening
according to their rules. . . .
               "We interrupt
this program. . . ."
               Inch by inch
the interruption overrules both worlds,
engulfing us like dustfall
from a building in collapse.
               The day
turns dark as an eclipse.
               We head
for home as if to be assured
that home is where we left it.

2.

Before both towers drowned
    in their own dust, someone

downfloated from the hundredth floor.
Then there were others—plunging,
     stepping off or diving in tandem,
     hand in hand, as if the sea
     or nets awaited them.
                    "My God,
     people are jumping!"
                    Of all
     the thousands there, we saw
     those few, just those, freefalling
     through the sky like flotsam from a blaze . . .
Nightmares of impact crushed us.
We slept like the doomed or drowned,
     then woke to oratory, vigils,
     valor, journalists declaring war
     and, snapping from aerials or poles,
     the furious clamor of flags.

Just Words

In Arabic a single word
     describes the very act
     of taking a position.
                    Greeks
     pronounce three syllables
     to signify the sense of doom
     that all Greeks fear when things
     are going very well.
                    As for
     the shameful ease we feel
     when bad news happens

to someone else, including
friends?
                    In Greek—one word.
To designate a hose that funnels
        liquid fire down the turret
        of a tank in battle, the Germans
        speak one word.
                            It's three
lines long but still one word.
And as for John, Matthew,
        Mark and Luke?
                        There's not
a surname in the lot.
                        With just
one name they match in memory
the immortality of martyrs.
                            The longer
they're dead, the more they live . . .
I praise whatever mates
        perception with precision!
                            It asks
us only to be spare and make
the most of least.
                        It simplifies
and lets each word sound final
as a car door being shut
but perfect as a telegram to God.

After Arlington

It lasts like a parade in place
  with only the essentials cut
  in rhyming white headstones:
  last names, initials,
  rank, branches of service.
The names answer up in a muster
  of silence while Washington's aglut
  with traffic, vectoring jets
  and disproportion.
        Maple groves,
  roadsigns and gardens
  remember Lady Bird and LBJ.
Facing the Department of Commerce,
  Reagan's billion-dollar
  palace rivals in square
  feet the whole damn Pentagon.
Roosevelt's granite marker,
  scaled as he asked to the length
  and width of his desk, is harder
  to find.
     Jack Kennedy,
  his widow, two children
  and his brother share one plot.
Across the slow Potomac,
  the names in black marble
  of 58,000 futile deaths
  consecrate less than an acre.

The First Sam Hazo at the Last

A minor brush with medicine
    in eighty years was all
    he'd known.
                But this was different.
His right arm limp and slung,
    his right leg dead to feeling
    and response, he let me spoon him
    chicken-broth.
              Later he said
without self-pity that he'd like
to die.
          I bluffed, "The doctors
think that therapy might help you
walk again."
            "They're liars,
all of them," he muttered.
                Bedfast
was never how he hoped to go.
"In bed you think of everything,"
    he whispered with a shrug, "you think
    of all of your life."
            I knew
he meant my mother.
              Without her
he was never what he might have been,
and everyone who loved him knew it.
Nothing could take her place—
    not the cars he loved to drive,
    not the money he could earn at will,
    not the roads he knew by heart

from Florida to Saranac, not the two
replacement wives who never
measured up.
              Fed now by family
or strangers, carried to the john,
shaved and changed by hired help,
this independent man turned silent
at the end.
              Only my wife
could reach him for his private needs.
What no one else could do
              for him, he let her do.
She talked to him and held
              his hand, the left.
                            She helped him
bless himself and prayed beside him
as my mother might have done.
"Darling" was his final word
              for her.
                            Softly, in Arabic.

The Mutineer

Leaves curl against the ground
    like Muslims at prayer.
                  In weeks
they'll change from elegies in place
into their own obituaries.
                  Now
they leave me leafing back,
back, back.
           My father meets me
on the way.
          At eighty he told me
he was shrinking.
          Lately, I've felt
the same, not physically, but otherwise.
The more I add the sum of all
    the living to the once alive,
    the more I seem to vanish
    in the balance.
           Watching the way
of leaves prefigures what I know
will come.
         It urges me
to take a flight to elsewhere
or make my creed defiance.
Meantime, I choose to mount
    my mutiny in words . . .
           Not much
as protests go, but something.

For Which It Stands

Crosswinds have slashed the flag
    so that the thirteenth ribbon
    dangles free or coils around
    the flagpole like a stripe.
                    What's left
    keeps fluttering in red-and-white
    defiance.
            Somehow the tattering
seems apropos.
              The President
    proclaims we'll be at war forever—
    not war for peace but war
    upon war, though hopefully not here.
Believers in eternal re-election
    hear his pitch and pay.
               In Washington
    God's lawyer warns we stand
    at Armageddon, and we battle
    for the Lord.
            Elsewhere, California's
    governor believes in California's
    governor, and football bowls
    are named for MasterCard, Pacific
    Life, ConAgra and Tostitos.
Out west a plan to gerrymander
    Colorado (Texas-style) fails,
    but barely.
           Asked why no flag
    is studded in his coat lapel
    or decorates his aerial, a veteran

responds, "I wear my flag
on my heart—I don't wear
my heart on my sleeve."
                                    Today
for once we're spared the names
of occupying soldiers shot
or rocketed to fragments in Iraq.
Collateral damage?
                        Two boys,
their mother and both grandparents.
No names for them . . .
                            Just Arabs.

Lawrence Joseph

Lawrence Joseph was born in Detroit, Michigan, in 1948. His grandparents, Lebanese and Syrian Catholics, were among the first Arab emigrants to Detroit. He earned degrees from the University of Michigan, the University of Cambridge, and the University of Michigan Law School. Before moving to New York City, where he practiced law and eventually joined the faculty at St. John's University School of Law, a position he has held since 1987, he served as law clerk to Justice G. Mennen Williams of the Michigan Supreme Court. Joseph has been called "the most important lawyer-poet of our era," and his poems have been described as "tough-minded, compassionate," and of "great dignity, grace, and unrelenting persuasiveness." His books include *Shouting at No One, Curriculum Vitae*, and *Before Our Eyes*—collected in *Codes, Precepts, Biases, and Taboos: Poems 1973–1993*—and a fourth collection, *Into It.* He is also the author of the prose book *Lawyerland.* Joseph's work has been widely anthologized, and his honors include fellowships from the John Simon Guggenheim Memorial Foundation, the National Endowment for the Arts, and the Agnes Lynch Starrett Prize. Married to the painter Nancy Van Goethem, he lives in downtown Manhattan.

It's Not Me Shouting at No One

Before dawn, on the street again,
beneath sky that washes me
with ice, smoke, metal.
I don't want to think
the bullet pierced my shoulder,
the junkie's rotten teeth
laughed, his yellow hair froze.
I'm careful: I smoke
Turkish tobacco cigarette butts,
I drink a lot to piss a lot,

I fry the pig in its own fat,
eat the knuckles, brain, and stomach;
I don't eat the eyes!
Always four smokestacks
burning bones, somewhere
tears that won't stop,
everywhere blood becomes
flesh that wants to say something.
It's not me shouting at no one
in Cadillac Square: it's God
roaring inside me, afraid
to be alone.

Do What You Can

In the Church of I AM she hears there is a time to heal,
but her son, Top Dog of the Errol Flynn gang,

doesn't lay down his sawed-off shotgun,
the corn she planted in the field where

the Marvel Motor Car factory once was
doesn't grow with pigweed and cocklebur.

When someone in the Resurrection Lounge laughs,
"Bohunk put the two-foot dogfish in the whore's hand,"

someone's daughter whispers, "Fuck you,"
places a half-smoked cigarette in her coat pocket,

swings open the thick wooden door and walks
into air that freezes when it hears frost

coming from Sault Sainte Marie. Driving, I see
a shed of homing pigeons, get out of my car to look.

I answer, "What you care?" to a woman who shouts, "What you want?"
Beside the Church of St. John Nepomocene

an old man, hunched and cold, prays, "Mother of God"
to a statue of the Virgin Mary

surrounded by a heart-shaped rosary
of fifty-three black and six white bowling balls.

Where the Ford and Chrysler freeways cross
a sign snaps, 5,142,250,

the number of cars produced so far this year in America.
Not far away, on Beaufait Street,

a crowd gathers to look at the steam
from blood spread on the ice. The light red,

I press the accelerator to keep the motor warm.
I wonder if they know

that after the jury is instructed
on the Burden of Persuasion and the Burden of Truth,

that after the sentence of twenty to thirty years comes down,
when the accused begs, "Lord, I can't do that kind of time,"

the judge, looking down, will smile and say,
"Then do what you can."

Curriculum Vitae

I might have been born in Beirut,
not Detroit, with my right name.
Grandpa taught me to love to eat.
I am not Orthodox, or Sunni,
Shiite, or Druse. Baptized
in the one true Church, I too
was weaned on Saint Augustine.
Eisenhower never dreamed I wore
corrective shoes. Ford Motor Co.
never cared I'd never forgive
Highland Park, River Rouge, Hamtramck.
I memorized the Baltimore Catechism.
I collected holy cards, prayed
to a litany of saints to intercede
on behalf of my father who slept
through the sermon at 7 o'clock Mass.
He worked two jobs, believed
himself a failure. My brother
believed himself, my sister denied.
In the fifth grade Sister Vicorine,
astonished, listened to me recite
from the Book of Jeremiah.
My voice changed. I wanted women.
The Jesuit whose yellow fingers
cracked with the stink of Camels
promised me eternal punishment.
How strange I was, with impure thoughts,
brown skin, obsessions.
You could tell by the way I walked
I possessed a lot of soul,
you could tell by the way I talked
I didn't know when to stop.

After I witnessed stabbings
outside the gym, after the game,
I witnessed fire in the streets.
My head set on fire in Cambridge,
England, in the Whim Café.
After I applied Substance and Procedure
and Statements of Facts
my head was heavy, was earth.
Now years have passed since I came
to the city of great fame.
The same sun glows gray on two new rivers.
Tears I want do not come.
I remain many different people
whose families populate half Detroit;
I hate the racket of the machines,
the oven's heat, curse
bossmen behind their backs.
I hear the inmates' collective murmur
in the jail on Beaubien Street.
I hear myself say, "What explains
the Bank of Lebanon's liquidity?"
think, "I too will declare
a doctrine upon whom the loss
of language must fall regardless
whether Wallace Stevens
understood senior indebtedness
in Greenwich Village in 1906."
One woman hears me in my sleep
plead the confusions of my dream.
I frequent the Café Dante, earn
my memories, repay my moods.
I am as good as my heart.
I am as good as the unemployed
who wait in long lines for money.

Sand Nigger

In the house in Detroit
in a room of shadows
when Grandma reads her Arabic newspaper
it is difficult for me to follow her
word by word from right to left
and I do not understand
why she smiles about the Jews
who won't do business in Beirut
"because the Lebanese
are more Jew than Jew,"
or whether to believe her
that if I pray
to the holy card of Our Lady of Lebanon
I will share the miracle.
Lebanon is everywhere
in the house: in the kitchen
of steaming pots, leg of lamb
in the oven, plates of kousa,
hushwee rolled in cabbage,
dishes of olives, tomatoes, onions,
roasted chicken, and sweets;
at the card table in the sunroom
where Grandpa teaches me
to wish the dice across the backgammon board
to the number I want;
Lebanon of mountains and sea,
of pine and almond trees,
of cedars in the service
of Solomon, Lebanon
of Babylonians, Phoenicians, Arabs, Turks

and Byzantines, of the one-eyed
monk, Saint Maron,
in whose rite I am baptized;
Lebanon of my mother
warning my father not to let
the children hear,
of my brother who hears
and from whose silence
I know there is something
I will never know; Lebanon
of Grandpa giving me my first coin
secretly, secretly
holding my face in his hands,
kissing me and promising me
the whole world.
My father's vocal cords bleed;
he shouts too much
at his brother, his partner,
in the grocery store that fails.
I hide money in my drawer, I have
the talent to make myself heard.
I am admonished to learn,
never to dirty my hands
with sawdust and meat.
At dinner, a cousin
describes his niece's head
severed with bullets, in Beirut,
in civil war. "More than
an eye for an eye," he demands,
breaks down, and cries.
My uncle tells me to recognize
my duty, to use my mind,

to bargain, to succeed.
He turns the diamond ring
on his finger, asks if
I know what asbestosis is,
"the lungs become like this,"
he says, holding up a fist;
he is proud to practice
law which "distributes
money to compensate flesh."
Outside the house my practice
is not to respond to remarks
about my nose or the color of my skin.
"Sand nigger," I'm called,
and the name fits: I am
the light-skinned nigger
with black eyes and the look
difficult to figure—a look
of indifference, a look to kill—
a Levantine nigger
in the city on the strait
between the great lakes Erie and St. Clair
which has a reputation
for violence, an enthusiastically
bad-tempered sand nigger
who waves his hands, nice enough
to pass, Lebanese enough
to be against his brother,
with his brother against his cousin,
with cousin and brother
against the stranger.

I Pay the Price

Memory slipping more and more,
whole days no longer exist.

It's not that I don't feel well.
Pulse 77, 76, I've learned

nothing will pass. Yesterday
the news full of dead,

the Dictionary on Historical Principles
open on the table

at the definition of "sentiment,"
today I hear market analysts

expectantly attend the latest
conferences on chaos.

Before the picture window vista
of the East River, I hear Miss

Newman—she insists she be called
Miss—expound her aesthetic.

"This city, the ultimate art!
Masses of steel and light

jutted beyond heaven, a miracle
that is human and works."

This city of my own, dull gray,
rose, yellow, murky pink skies.

I know what I'm saying. I know
tomorrow I may forget

the man whom I see tonight
on Pearl Street under the Bridge

who appears at first to have no head.
He asks me to tell him

who he is, to take him, please,
to the police. He is sick,

mentally. He hasn't controlled
his bladder or his bowels.

Tomorrow I've also a big day ahead of me
protecting interests.

Though I don't have the appropriate letters
to get where I want,

my progress continues.
I distance myself to see myself

say to myself even before
I hang up the telephone, "I love this!"

From my apartment, from which I've a good view
of the same Bridge, I watch

a workman standing on the pier, looking
across at the coast turning toward

the Narrows, his hands bandaged,
victim of a work accident

who doesn't know what to think
or what to do and hasn't enough

to buy himself something to settle his mind.
I walk about my rooms

composing arguments in my defense.
"Live and die before a mirror,"

Baudelaire says, sipping espresso
at the corner of Hudson and Barrow.

I live in words and off my flesh
in order to pay the price.

When the ancient fury persists,
I pay the price.

Before Our Eyes

The sky almost transparent, saturated
manganese blue. Windy and cold.
A yellow line beside a black line,
the chimney on the roof a yellow line
behind the mountain ash on Horatio.
A circular cut of pink flesh hanging
in the shop. Fish, flattened, copper,
heads chopped off. The point is to bring
depths to the surface, to elevate
sensuous experience into speech
and the social contract. Ribbons on smoke
silhouette the pier, a navy of yachts
pounded by the river's green waves.

By written I mean made, by made I mean felt;
concealed things, sweet sleep of colors.
So you will be, perhaps appropriately,
dismissed for it, a morality of seeing,
laying it on. Who among the idealists
won't sit in the private domain,
exchange culture with the moneymakers?
Here's one with acute hypertension
ready to crack the pressure cuff,
there's the type whose hallucinatory
devolution of the history of tribes
is personalized. My grandpa? He never
contended where Lebanon's history
began, if the child prince was smuggled
by his mother to a Catholic family
in the Mountain where he passed his boyhood
in his father's religion, a Druse,
the most secret sect of Islam.
I received the news in Jerusalem—
the Beirut Easter radio event, the dancer
undulating to sounds of explosions
outside the studio. The future isn't Africa,
my friend, and Europe's a peninsula of Asia,
and your America's a creation of Europe,
he laughed, the newspaperman, pointing
his finger. Still, don't street smarts
matter? Waiting rooms, shopping centers,
after all, empty moods and emotions.
And no denial's built up inside me.
It was, I admit, more charged than
I thought at the time. More predetermined.
Silver and red scraps inside the air,

cascades of sublimated pig iron.
Language more discursive, a more sequential
expression, and I attested to it.
The old dying? The new not yet born? The old,
the new, you fool, aphorized by Henry Ford
in '22. First make the cars, the roads
will follow. Modes of production created
of their own accord. The process runs
of its own accord. Current and diaphanous
sight and sound, comprehended, but poetry
I know something about. The act of forming
imagined language resisting humiliation.
Fading browns and reds, a maroon glow,
sadness and brightness, glorified.
Voices over charred embankments, smell
of fire and fat. The pure metamorphic
rush through with senses, just as you said
it would be. The soft, subtle twilight
only the bearer feels, broken into angles,
best kept to oneself. For the time being
let's just keep to what's before our eyes.

Rubaiyat

The holes burned in the night.
Holes you can look through and see
the stump of a leg, a bloody
bandage, flies on the gauze; a pulled-up

satellite image of a major
military target, a 3-D journey
into a landscape of hills and valleys . . .

All of it from real-world data.

Zoom in close enough—the shadows
of statues, the swimming pools of palaces . . .
closer—a garden of palm trees,
oranges and lemons, chickens, sheep;

a map being sketched on a scrap
of paper; a fist coming down firmly
on the table; a tray with a dish
of lamb, and a bowl of rice and pine nuts.

Yes, that's it. I've become
too clear-sighted—the mechanics of power
are too transparent. Yes, that's
precisely it. The creation

of a deep-down pit, a slag heap
of broken masonry, of twisted metal,
a persistent ringing noise from inside—
as if thousands of telephones have been

left off the hook. Did you notice that?
The Pentagon's "Military Diaries
Project," soldiers starring in their own
war movies, training digital cameras

on themselves—a child is put
in a wheelbarrow after stepping on a mine.
Politics? Personified. His head
permanently cocked, he is attended

by a team of physicians
and an electronic-implant engineer.

He hopes he'll be able to confer
with the Shah of Iran in Cairo. "Dead?

The Shah? Really? No one's said a thing
to me about it," his response to the response
of a diplomatic press correspondent.
Poetry's not what's made impossible

by it—laughter is. Is it even
farce?—the translator, for example, who,
because of threats, is wearing a bulletproof
vest and a large pair of army goggles

for disguise, the sniper who slides
a condom over the muzzle of his gun
to keep the sand out. I try to get
the chronology straight . . . I look

out on the harbor, in the blue light.
I type into my machine. Perhaps
a glance at the newspaper. I listen
closely and I don't listen at all . . .

How complicated do you think the geopolitical
background behind all of this is? Brains
uprooted and warped, the logic's
schizophrenic. What's that again? A poem,

a speech, of lament, a threnody.
A poem of thoughts, of consequences.
Time flows, is flowing, forward and back.
I lift a spoon, my hand is trembling. How many

corpses are counted and for what reasons?
That's what was said. The captured are blinded
except one blinded in one eye only
will lead the others back. What? War

as a living text? Cyberwar and permanent
war, Third Wave War, neocortical war,
Sixth Generation War, Fourth Epoch
War, pure war and war of computers

to process it, systems
to represent it, war of myth
and metaphor, of trope and assent,
war of hundreds of millions of televisions

assuring it, hundreds of billions
of dollars, a PK machine gun or two, a few
gunmen you can hire cheap, with their own
Kalashnikovs. Now . . . what now?

I want you to watch carefully
what I am saying now—are you
with me? An inch-long piece of steel,
part of the artillery shell's

casing, sliced through the right eye
into his brain, severely damaging
the optic nerve of his left eye,
spraying bone splinters

into the brain, making him quick to lose
his temper, so acutely sensitive to pain
the skin on his face hurts
when wind blows against it . . .

Inclined to Speak

I saw that. One woman, her personality
and appearance described as lovely,
while performing her predawn prayers,
watched the attackers shoot to death her husband,
her seven-year-old son, three of her brothers,
as they grabbed her four-year-old son from her arms
and cut his throat, taking her and her two sisters
away on horses and raping them. Of course it's genocide.
And, yes, it brings to mind I am constantly aware of,
in making the poem, Brecht's point, to write about trees—
implicitly, too, to write about pleasure—
in times of killing like these is a crime;
and Paul Celan's response, that for Brecht a leaf
is a leaf without a tree, that what kinds of times
are these when a conversation—Celan believed a poem
is a conversation—what kinds of times are these
when a poem is a crime because it includes
what must be made explicit.

                            What is seen, heard, and imagined
at the same time—that truth. A sort of relationship
is established between our attention
to what is furthest from us
and what deepest in us. The immense enlargement
of our perspectives is confronted
by a reduction in our powers of action, which reduces
a voice to an inner voice inclined to speak only
to those closest to us . . .

Fady Joudah

A physician with Doctors without Borders, Fady Joudah was selected by Louise Glück for the Yale Younger Poets prize for his first book, *The Earth in the Attic*. His poems have appeared in such journals as the *Beloit Poetry Journal,* the *Kenyon Review,* and *Prairie Schooner* and have received numerous awards and nominations, including the River City Poetry Award and the Pushcart Prize. He is also a translator. Of Mahmoud Darwish's *The Butterfly's Burden,* Marilyn Hacker writes that in Joudah, "Darwish has found a translator capable of rendering in English his unflinching, questing, and above all loving poems." Joudah lives in Houston, Texas.

Morning Ritual

Every morning, after the roosters
Crow back whatever prayers were passed
Down to them that dawn
From the keeper of their order up in heaven,

I drink my coffee
To the sound of squealing pigs
Being bled to death
In the market up the road—the same market

Where I buy my fresh bread
For my peanut butter and jam. The pigs
Are bled through an armpit wound.
You can see it coming throughout the day before,

Hogs tied sideways to the backs of bicycles,
Tight as a spine, going as far as the border
Where the price is right. You will pass them
On the asphalt to the town I get

The peanut butter and jam from. They know
The bikeways out of nowhere
And suddenly they're alongside your jeep.
I lie: only goats are taken to the border.

The goats are bled differently,
And skinning is harmless after slaughter:
All you do is a vertical skin-slit
Between the shinbone and Achilles' tendon,

Stick a thin metal rod
Through it, up the thigh, pull it out
Then blow, mouth to hole,
Until your breath dehisces

Fascia and dermis, reaching the belly:
Your hands
Should even out the trapped air.
Between blowing and tapping

The animal is tight as a drum.
Now the knife that slit the throat.
Who knows
What you'll need skin for.

At a Café

I am still a Mohammedan hunched like a gibbous moon and veiled:
outside, a woman who speaks clearly in order to be heard, right
out of the parlor, nails trimmed and polished, afraid to pop open
her diet Pepsi and damage the cuticles. I use my own teeth-
trimmed nails instead, and she thanks me. We're at a café, not a
mosque. And she makes it back safe to her jaguar, cell-phone in
one hand and a sip in the other, speaking about the stone in the
middle of her heart. The pain doesn't radiate to the left shoulder,
neck or jaw. The pain never causes her to break out in a sweat.
Which means, I can do nothing about it. And the stone is so huge
and exophytic only her legs and arms are visible. She's a beetle
flipped on her back, stone fungating out of her ribs. Nothing can
hide her now, not even a Trojan horse.

Sleeping Trees

Between what should and what should not be
Everything is liable to explode. Many times
I was told *who has no land has no sea.* My father
Learned to fly in a dream. This is the story
Of a sycamore tree he used to climb
When he was young to watch the rain.

Sometimes it rained so hard it hurt. Like being
Beaten with sticks. Then the mud would run red.

My brother believed bad dreams could kill
A man in his sleep, he insisted
We wake my father from his muffled screams
On the night of the day he took us to see his village.
No longer his village he found his tree amputated.
Between one falling and the next

There's a weightless state. There was a woman
Who loved me. Asked me how to say *tree*
In Arabic. I didn't tell her. She was sad. I didn't understand.
When she left, I saw a man in my sleep three times. A man I knew
Could turn anyone into one-half reptile.
I was immune. I thought I was. I was terrified of being

The only one left. When we woke my father
He was running away from soldiers. Now
He doesn't remember that night. He laughs
About another sleep, he raised his arms to strike a king
And tried not to stop. He flew
But mother woke him and held him for an hour,

Or half an hour, or as long as it takes a migration inward.
Maybe if I had just said it,

Shejerah, she would've remembered me longer. Maybe
I don't know much about dreams
But my mother taught me the law of omen. The dead
Know about the dying and sometimes
Catch them in sleep like the sycamore tree
My father used to climb

When he was young to watch the rain stream,
And he would gently swing.

Additional Notes on Tea

In Cairo a boy's balcony higher than a man's deathbed.

The boy is sipping tea,

The view is angular like a fracture.

Surrounding the bed, women in wooden chairs.

They signal mourning with a scream.

Family men on the street run up the stairs and drink raven tea.

On the operating table in Solwezi a doctor watches a woman die.

Tea while the anesthetic wears off,

While the blade is waiting, tea.

The doctor says the woman knows god is sleeping

Outside heaven in a tent.

God is a refugee dreaming of tea.

Once upon a time an ocean married a sea to carry tea around.

Land was jealous.

So it turned into desert and gave no one wood for ships.

And when ships became steel,

Land turned into ice.

And when everything melted, everything tasted like tea.

Once upon a time there was a tea party in Boston.

Tea, like history, is a non sequitur.

I prefer it black. The Chinese drink it green.

Mohja Kahf

Mohja Kahf's poetry "offers articulate, passionate challenges to commonplace perceptions" of the Middle East and its people, striking "notes of humor, compassion, outrage and celebration that resonate across the literary register." Throughout her writings—she is the author of a poetry book, *E-mails from Scheherazad;* a novel, *The Girl in the Tangerine Scarf;* and a scholarly book, *Western Representations of the Muslim Woman from Termagant to Odalisque*—she shows a keen eye for the "creative dissonance of seemingly incongruous juxtapositions." Born in Damascus, Syria, she now teaches comparative literature at the University of Arkansas.

My Grandmother Washes Her Feet in the Sink of the Bathroom at Sears

My grandmother puts her feet in the sink
    of the bathroom at Sears
to wash them in the ritual washing for prayer,
wudu,
because she has to pray in the store or miss
the mandatory prayer time for Muslims
She does it with great poise, balancing
herself with one plump matronly arm
against the automated hot-air hand dryer,
after having removed her support knee-highs
and laid them aside, folded in thirds,
and given me her purse and her packages to hold
so she can accomplish this august ritual
and get back to the ritual of shopping for housewares

Respectable Sears matrons shake their heads and frown
as they notice what my grandmother is doing,

an affront to American porcelain,
a contamination of American Standards
by something foreign and unhygienic
requiring civic action and possible use of disinfectant spray
They fluster about and flutter their hands and I can see
a clash of civilizations brewing in the Sears bathroom

My grandmother, though she speaks no English,
catches their meaning and her look in the mirror says,
I have washed my feet over Iznik tile in Istanbul
with water from the world's ancient irrigation systems
I have washed my feet in the bathhouses of Damascus
over painted bowls imported from China
among the best families of Aleppo
And if you Americans knew anything
about civilization and cleanliness,
you'd make wider washbasins, anyway
My grandmother knows one culture—the right one,

as do these matrons of the Middle West. For them,
my grandmother might as well have been squatting
in the mud over a rusty tin in vaguely tropical squalor,
Mexican or Middle Eastern, it doesn't matter which,
when she lifts her well-groomed foot and puts it over the edge.
"You can't do that," one of the women protests,
turning to me, "Tell her she can't do that."
"We wash our feet five times a day,"
my grandmother declares hotly in Arabic.
"My feet are cleaner than their sink.
Worried about their sink, are they? I
should worry about my feet!"
My grandmother nudges me, "Go on, tell them."

Standing between the door and the mirror, I can see
at multiple angles, my grandmother and the other shoppers,
all of them decent and goodhearted women, diligent
in cleanliness, grooming, and decorum
Even now my grandmother, not to be rushed,
is delicately drying her pumps with tissues from her purse
For my grandmother always wears well-turned pumps
that match her purse, I think in case someone
from one of the best families of Aleppo
should run into her—here, in front of the Kenmore display

I smile at the midwestern women
as if my grandmother has just said something lovely about them
and shrug at my grandmother as if they
had just apologized through me
No one is fooled, but I

hold the door open for everyone
and we all emerge on the sales floor
and lose ourselves in the great common ground
of housewares on markdown

Hijab Scene #1

"You dress strange," said a tenth-grade boy with bright blue hair
to the new Muslim girl with the headscarf in homeroom,
his tongue-rings clicking on the "tr" in "strange."

Hijab Scene #2

"You people have such restrictive dress for women,"
she said, hobbling away in three-inch heels and panty hose
to finish out another pink-collar temp pool day.

Postcards from Hajar, a Correspondence in Four Parts

> *O our Lord, I have made some of my family to dwell in a valley without*
> *cultivation by your sacred House . . . so fill the hearts of some people with*
> *love for them, and provide fruit for them that they may give thanks*
> —The prayer of Abraham (Quran, Ibrahim:37)

i.

Ismaïl and I made it,
in case you're wondering.
Been learning the basics
of wilderness survival.
Weather very hot here,
but it's a dry heat,
bearable
once you find a water supply.
Angel Gabe dropped by,
fixed plumbing
so we have a well.
We're invited to the Jurhum's tonight

for dinner with the tribe.
Their girl
is Ismaïl's age.
Tell Sarah I said—
oh, never mind.
Regards,
Hajar
P.s. I have decided to found a nation.

ii.

Sarah's pregnant, wish you were here
to talk her through it.
We often think of you
and how it used to be
when you and the baby were with us.
It wasn't so bad, was it? Helpmeet
you were, to a lonely aging couple,
and so bright you filled the house.
Glad to know you two survived
abandonme—er, being in the desert.
Nice to hear about the water and all.
A nation, huh? Well, you take care.
Hugs to Ismaïl. Write back soon!
Fondly, your ex,
Abraham

iii.

The baby is moving.
I'm too old for this! (laughing)
I will teach him to love his big brother.
Maybe one day they will
make up for their mothers.
Look, I'm sorry things went the way

they did between us, Hajar.
It just wasn't working.
In the end, it was my marriage and
I had to save it. I am relieved
things are all right for you
over there in that—that distant
—well, that place where you went.
You and your son will always
have a place in my regard.
Sincerely,
Sarah

iv.

Been busier and busier, hard
to find time to write, what with
our new city, my responsibilities
as founding mother.
Ismaïl sends love to baby
brother Isaac (congratulations!).
Sarah, yes, breastfeeding is tough
on nipples at first but keep at it.
You will see in his brown eyes
dreams of warm milk
and still the hoarse hyena
of a deadly hunger.
Abraham, if you do
drop by sometime, we
may well have increased
like unto the starry sky
and multiplied.
Peace,
Hajar

Pauline Kaldas

Pauline Kaldas, born in Egypt, immigrated with her parents to the United States in 1969, at the age of eight. She is the author of *Egyptian Compass*, a collection of poetry, and *Letters from Cairo*, a travel memoir, and the coeditor of *Dinarzad's Children: An Anthology of Contemporary Arab American Fiction*. Her work has appeared in a variety of journals and anthologies, including *Phoebe, Borderlands, The Poetry of Arab Women, Cultural Activisms,* and *The Space between Our Footsteps*. She was also awarded a fellowship in fiction from the Virginia Commission for the Arts. She holds a Ph.D. from Binghamton University and teaches literature and creative writing at Hollins University in Roanoke, Virginia.

Bird Lessons

"You will find it in the soup"
   the bowl with steam turning to clouds
into shapes   My friends cringe as they fish
with their spoon net
   but no petals of flesh are caught
     only pilaf noodles that narrow on each end
"We call them bird's tongue because of the shape
you will find them in the soup"
Their eyes look down
   they had expected something exotic
     and would have preferred pink flesh

but it is I who cringe
   we are not savages   I am blind
by pink tongues flapping in my broth

pink tongues flapping in my broth they paddle to stay alive propel from one side to the other what if they jump and flap a slap across my face? I put them in boiling broth expand them to their greatest potential they are noodles and I am obsessed with their name why should pasta tamer than alphabets have such a vicious name? the bird left with gaping hoarse beak put up your fists you phrase maker we have letters to settle I grew up with my grandmother putting them in my vegetable soup my mother in chicken soup and I in clear broth how dare you give a name with color shall giants cut my tongue to flavor their soup and do men who turn cannibal eat the round soft point you touch the tip of your nose with? what kind of tongue do the dead have thin flat or with zigzag cuts like my last lover? how to treat these noodles in my broth will they grow to giants *lesan el asfour lesan* tongue *el* of *asfour* bird a tiny bird forced to put in my soup explain to dinner guests what is in their bowls or when I send a stranger to shop no other translation and I am blind with birds flapping in my broth.

Fraudulent Acts

to be walking on the Nile corniche
nostalgia bordered by sticky smog of polluted air
to hail a cab, negotiate a fare
        hold the silent façade   of being Egyptian
who impersonates
    walking through a Nubian village
people guess: "he's Egyptian you're Foreigner"
the waiter in Falfela taking me for a European woman

But once in Siwa a young man recognizes I am Coptic
"it was your eyes"
the first time I imagine my religion
        shadowed on my features
           like a palm tree carries
           its ripened yellow dates
Maggie tells me Copts have big round eyes, small chins
I search out faces   decipher the lines that draw us

At the spring fed pond near desert edge,
where soon an Italian company will build a luxury hotel
advertising the healing waters of Siwa,
a young boy assures "Copts are bad and must die"

taken to where

*there was a woman who found herself drowning in the water while carrying
her child. desperate because the child had not been baptized and death was near,
she said in the name of the father and son and baptized the child herself in the
sea's water. after she was rescued, she went to the church, but every time the
priest lowered her child to the basin, the water dried up. three times this
happened until the priest asked her if this child had ever been baptized before.
the woman confessed and told him what had happened. and the priest said,
God has accepted your baptism.*

having carried
this story against so many doubts

"So you'll have to wear a veil"
a breath to inhale to explain
overlooking heads: anyone with uncovered hair now suspect
likely to be Coptic
taken for what   at the airport's glass enclosure
aren't you Egyptian why the passport stamped Tourist?

My Aunt's Kitchen

Cupboard open to rows of glass jars, wax paper lines the lids to close tightly, filled with pickled lemons, beets, peppers, onions; tangerine jam, date jam, grape jam; old cheese in mixture of oil and lemon marinates its taste more pungent daily. Every day, filling clay olas with water, saving empty jars on one side and on the other their mismatched lids to fit later. My uncle's house laid out neatly. He tells me: one side for winter, enclosed porch, no windows look east and light through screens enters heavily; the other side a summer porch, screens unobstructed look over the house of the man who owns *Kentucky Fried Chicken*; in his garden, a young servant girl, hair kerchiefed, follows a dog.

What America Has to Offer

How wonderful this thing they call the supermarket:
cans of fruit salad and pineapple,
graham cracker cookies, frozen vegetables,
dried onions and garlic, canned tomato paste!
Those hours spent washing, cutting, peeling vegetables,
making tomato sauce from tomatoes. Only
a can, poured into a pot, a little water
and you were done?

This is indeed America, the land of miracles.
The men declare: it doesn't taste the same;
they want the long hot day, peeling and chopping
onions and garlic, frying, the smell of *taelia*
to greet them when they come home.

Let them feed themselves.
And the women begin to share secrets
on the back of cake mixes.

Lisa Suhair Majaj

A Palestinian American, Lisa Suhair Majaj is the author of two poetry chapbooks, *These Words* and *What She Said.* Her poems "remind us what it is to be human," utilizing a variety of "ways of knowing," from the lyrical to the political, the historical to the spiritual. A widely published poet, Majaj is also one of the United States' foremost scholars of Arab American literature and has coedited three collections of critical essays. Born in a small Iowa farming town to an American mother and a Palestinian father, Majaj moved several times between the United States and the Middle East. She now lives in Nicosia, Cyprus.

In Season

My father knew the weight of words
in balance, stones in a weathered wall.

He counseled patience,
though, dying, refused his own

advice. Today his words surround me
with the quiet intensity

of growing things, roots planted a long time ago
lacing the distances of my heart.

What he didn't say is sprouting too,
a surprise, like the *eskidinya* tree

that sprang from the smooth brown pit
I tossed off the porch as a child.

Years now I've longed to pick that fruit—
remembering how he'd sit

spitting seeds in a stream to the ground—
but I know it's not yet ripe. So I think,

instead, of the lemon tree
in my uncle's yard. When it died,

no one could bear to cut it down.
They lopped off the branches,

but kept the dead trunk, stumps
of arms upraised—each bearing,

like bird's nests, a potted plant.
Out of habit, they still water the trunk,

and as if in return, each branch sparks green—
though every heart's separate, now,

not like the lemons that used to cluster
like triple suns. Did my parents know

that what they planted,
roots against the drought,

would survive? Today,
I'm a stump of a branch.

But on my tongue a seed
lies dormant, dense with life.

Unspoken years
fill my mouth like citrus

in winter—sharp promise
of sun. Outside, *eskidinya*

hang heavy as memory,
orange flash from dusty leaves,

their season still ripening.

It Wasn't Poetry

it wasn't poetry, those years
(summer toothsome as a ripe fruit,
juice dripping down our wrists)

it was trees and shadows
pieces of wind blown in from the sea
boats and waves and bodies

it was the passion moon
yellow as a smoker's tooth
palms pressed red against the sky

it was voices climbing atop each other
like crazed people in a locked room,
a child's wail pulled from a private place

it was moonlight pooling on the concrete,
long oars of light,
the silver odor of blood

it was sentinels falling, dregs of desperation,
ceasefire seizing the streets,
and the future, lifetimes away,

dreaming us safe

Arguments

consider the infinite fragility of an infant's skull,
how the bones lie soft and open
only time knitting them shut

consider a delicate porcelain bowl
how it crushes under a single blow—
in one moment whole years disappear

consider: beneath the din of explosions
no voice can be heard
no cry

consider your own sky on fire
your name erased
your children's lives "a price worth paying"

consider the faces you do not see
the eyes you refuse to meet
"collateral damage"

how in these words
the world
cracks open

I Remember My Father's Hands

because they were large, and square
fingers chunky, black hair like wire

because they fingered worry beads over and over
(that muted clicking, that constant motion, that secular prayer)

because they ripped bread with quiet purpose
dipped fresh green oil like a birthright

because after his mother's funeral they raised a tea cup
set it down untouched, uncontrollably trembling

because when they trimmed hedges, pruned roses
their tenderness caught my breath with jealousy

because once when I was a child they cupped my face
dry and warm, flesh full and calloused, for a long moment

because over his wife's still form they faltered
great mute helpless beasts

because when his own lungs filled and sank they reached out
for the first time pleading

because when I look at my hands
his own speak back

Jack Marshall

Jack Marshall was born in 1936 in Brooklyn, New York, to an Iraqi father and a Syrian mother. He is the author of several poetry volumes, including *Gorgeous Chaos: New + Selected Poems 1965–2001* and *Sesame*, winner of the PEN Center West Literary Award and a National Book Critics Circle Award finalist. "Supple and mystical," Marshall's poems are marked by an "unadorned nakedness." In addressing the "cities and cultures that shaped his artistic awakening," including the complexities of his Arab Jewish upbringing, his poems "hit their target dead center." His memoir, *From Baghdad to Brooklyn*, was named a finalist for the PEN USA Award in 2006. Marshall, who has taught at the Iowa Writers' Workshop, now lives in San Francisco.

Walking Across Brooklyn Bridge

A black cat arching its back over the river
was how it looked that time, that first
time years ago, sailing out
from under. Behind me, hazy
as litter freshly-flushed, a string
of furnished rooms yawned
toward the Heights, the house
I couldn't love and gave up trying;
the cemetery next door, like a rough diamond
crystallizing, stone by crowning stone,
to a cutting-edge perfection,
where I used to walk, listening
for my own shadow, thin,
and bloated with moonlight, still too thin,
slipping through the bars, in and out,
stitching me in place.

Leaving was all I knew then. . . .

A stowaway sneaking brief, shallow breaths
under pitchblack tarpaulin,
his eye, a fingernail
picking at a patch of pale blue sky
big as a postage stamp,
trying to think what his rights were,
getting nowhere. . . .

Today, March twenty-first,
ten years, not too late, but later,
I walk across with the girl
you'd spoken against, who is my wife,
taking it all in:
light, through The Narrows' neck, unbottling,
erasing the shadow that circles me;
this bridge, sung to once
as a sort of lover or god.
And though I do not claim as much,
I can feel us breathing
great, reviving drafts of North Atlantic air,
the steel-ribbed diaphragm
humming like a harp.

Below us, taking their slow, sweet time,
three tugs drag in a tramper;
demurring, blistered down to waterline,
giving a toot for Liberty,
it keeps on coming in.
I would have you know,
in spite of our words, our silences,
and though I do not understand or love it,
I accept my life.

Appalachia Suite

Winter not yet gone
from the stone, and churchbells chime
"Summertime, and the livin' is easy"
over the heads of the poor, reborn
each morning for the appetite of cities.
What windows there are, open
to slag-hill shadows inside of which no one sees
their own shadow. Cancelled by half,
scented with soot, where the dust slows your spit
down the backyard cinderpath, somewhere
between dew and dynamo young kids cuff
the mouths of Coke bottles with their palms, releasing
a moan as close as they'll ever come
to foghorns, and holding on to
the hopeless light of the past holding fast
to the hopeful light to come, all golden
promises tomorrow is already antiqued with . . .
While their fathers wrestle blocks of anthracite
and feel the urge to commit petty larceny
subside in the glow of the weekly paycheck;
and their sisters, gone west, find
the glowing lights are still further on,
and what lasts is what was spoken last
at home: "Let your heart hold us in,"
even as the lights there go out.

Crane

Tonight I want to return to Elizabeth,
New Jersey, where Stephen Crane lies
under a stone, and my father,
after twenty years of skimping wages, finally
opened his own dry-goods store.
I worked there after school, on weekends,
but it didn't take a genius to see
from the sad look of the place—
dim light, threadbare "goods"—where it was headed.
In all the time I spent in that smog-sucking town
of wan bargain hunters and hangdog merchants,
I never knew of, let alone visited,
Crane's grave. Then, I was more enamored of
that other Crane, Hart (lovely name!),
whose grave is the belly of the South Atlantic.
Besides, I couldn't imagine any reason why
anyone would want to stop off, never mind
die, in Elizabeth, New Jersey. It seemed
nobody there cared about, much less
knew, the color of the sky.

G—D

Is how we unspelled it back then, taboo-
Loaded, defused for secular use,
While the rabbis, all beard and black cloth, hovered

Overhead, gall-breathed, stick-wielding
Watchdogs shadowing the pages we scrawled on
Omitting the one-

Forbidden o-
Void vowel, hollow
Between consonantal poles, short-

Circuiting powers of the unutterable
Name the eye does not reach and words turn back from

Together with the mind.

· · ·

Those raised, ready sticks—broad as two-by-fours—
Pried from the backs of hardwood chairs, struck
Open palms, clenched fists, deep stinging

Whacks if you lost your place in the reading of the sacred text.
One summer day, dodging a random blow, a headstrong boy
Leaped out the classroom window to the ground

Two floors below, picked himself up with a curse
We'd utter only under our breath

And hobbled off, never to return.

· · ·

Ancestral, perennial, penitential,
Bred-in-the-blood diet
Of denials, feeding
On exile's endless
Minus sign, subtraction
Of all feeling but the mute

Recognition: before the first step is taken,
The end is reached; before the tongue moves,

Speech is finished.

· · ·

I can even now hardly bring myself
To spell it whole, so fiercely
Did those scowling fanatics guard against the invisible

From taking form.

• • •

Ha-shem, we said in Hebrew, meaning the Holy Name.
But in English the veiled vacancy more visibly
Renders the withheld power of what is not there.

Chaos—down to the microscopic
Mess of atomic elements and molecular mayhem—is ordered
Creation compared to that minuscule black

Slot housing wormhole loops and branches bridging
Worlds lost to us down micro-networks of space and time,
As many as there are

Motions, motion creating forms, forms
In motion, constantly
Deforming, reforming

Singularities just below a horizon
All depth but not yet
Given birth to light.

• • •

What might you have said
Had you been allowed to
Speak? What might you have thought

Had you been allowed to think?
And, forgetting what you were supposed to
Know, what knowledge might not flow

And, like all pleasure and science that heals, fly
In the face of Tables of the Law?

• • •

Unapprehendable, unapproachable
Creator of the universe permanently

Out of the galactic lariat
Loop that filling in would cinch and knot: the nothing
If-not-worlds-wanton

Original ovum
Circled by astral tadpoles
Drilling to the core . . .

Though no Rimbaud, this I know:
O echoes,
Enlarging space, its mother—

Moaning *A* beginning to brim
Molecular messengers already
Full-grown bodies on the nuclear lattice . . .

Hung by a thread, the moment
Opening them to the tame household deities
Opens to the whirlwind

Gods that have no name.

The Home-Front

After the pin-
point fraction of concentrated hell-
fire is reined in and the generals

call off their air war on Baghdad, concrete-and-steel
rosette Babylonian garden
in the desert of my father's birth nearly wiped

from the earth, we watch
ragged, runny-nosed street Arabs
underneath aureoles of filthy curls

playing with live ammo in a minefield's mud,
their faces a play
of glance, grin, grimacing

moves too intent on their games to choose
caution over curiosity. . . . Torrid
sunlight is their only nutrient.

Turning to the camera, their wide
eyes withdraw, filling with darkness
against the light off the dunes.

If eyes don't lie,
who will not see his own
child's face in theirs, stark

beauty of things in peril, more alarmingly
alive looking out of the ditch
than we looking in?—the Law

like a loaded gun trained on them.
Who, if he could, would give up his seat
and go down and look

through those eyes at the darkness so suddenly
fallen, Abraham's knife still
slicing the air down

the blue sky their bodies would be made of
if only the absentee Lord
God, against all evidence, were to return, bewitch

sweet water from the salty sea
and create us right for once?
Promises and prayers come

to nothing. Each day we act against our blood-
bond with the other side and manage to hide
the shame of having abandoned it. . . .

Such is the scent of the sulfurous
present on the home-front:
everything racing at increasing speed

toward the opposite of what we intended.

Place in the Real

1.

There was (or is?) a colonel on my father's side—
he once showed me a photo of
in *The New York Times*, must have been

late 1940s. Picture with me if you will
a Bedouin-kin, baked stoic
look in a lean face, earnest gaze,

much like a younger version of my father
with the added dash of a military-bar mustache
above the tailored uniform of the Iraqi elite corps—
uncle? cousin? nephew?—who
knew? In the time it takes to
glance and register a node

of hardly any interest to a boy,
I noted the family face, like an echo
visible down the ages, and looked away,

taking in as little as I could then.

2.

It comes
as no surprise: the older you get
the further back it takes

to reach some bare,
buried note
no matter how random or remote

a recognition or fleeting
trace.

> Except for an obscure
oddball uncle or two, we hardly knew
his side. . . . He didn't offer,

we didn't pursue—not unusual
for a boy whose total consuming mental effort
was: not to be there. Families are to flee from. . . .

3.

In the cyanide light of recent events,
I wonder what became of him: did the high command
know he was a Jew?

Might he have survived the cabals, purges, coups
that periodically irrigate
those blood-thirsty Biblical sands?
If he converted to other
than the double masquerade of the Marranos,
did he pass, or what loopholes slip through?

All that is moot.
As with the rest of his clan, I never asked
or gave him a thought.

In the annulling anonymity of time that makes us
all the same age at once, little more than
a pang says he has most likely been erased

from human eyes. When mine last saw his,
he could have been anyone—anonymous
as an atom—as my father is and I will be,

so that if only for the moment it takes
to tell of hardly
any difference between a possible life, partly

mine, and certain extinction, which is everyone's,
let this memory pass as virtual
elegy and its fleeting

(as his life most likely long since did)
take place in the real.

Khaled Mattawa

Born in Benghazi, Libya, Khaled Mattawa immigrated to the United States in 1979 at age fifteen. He lived in the South for many years, completing high school in Louisiana and earning degrees from the University of Tennessee at Chattanooga and from Indiana University. Of his first poetry book, Stanley Moss wrote that it would be "an oversimplification to say that *Ismailia Eclipse* . . . joins the literature of exiled poets." His second book, *Zodiac of Echoes*, was described as "one of the most compelling portraits we have of a mind, a sensibility, a language emerging from the hybridization of cultures." Mattawa, coeditor of *Post Gibran: Anthology of New Arab American Writing* and of *Dinarzad's Children: An Anthology of Contemporary Arab American Fiction*, has also translated five volumes of Arabic poetry. A recipient of many honors, including a fellowship from the John Simon Guggenheim Memorial Foundation, the Alfred Hodder Fellowship from Princeton University, and a National Endowment for the Arts translation grant, he teaches at the University of Michigan at Ann Arbor.

Growing Up with a Sears Catalog in Benghazi, Libya

Omar pointed to a pink man
riding a red lawn mower,
rose bushes, yellow tulips,
orchids framing slick sod.
Owners of villas in Jilyana,
my brother's friends
desperately needed
"the grass machines."
He planned to charge triple
his cost, build a house
by the sea. Eyes half-shut,
cigarette clouds above him,

he snored leaving unfinished
a recitation of truncated schemes.
In my room I gazed
at the pink man again,
marveled at pictures
of women in transparent bras.
How I loved their black nipples
and full gray breasts!
I fancied camping
with the blue-eyed one
in the $42 Coleman tent,
the two of us fishing
at a lake without mosquitoes,
sailing the boat on page 613.
After watching soaps
on our mahogany-cased
(27 inch) color TV,
we galloped in lime green scooters
on "scabrous terrain,"
returned to our 4-bedroom home,
mud up to our knees,
to make love on the mattress
on page 1219.

One morning,
my brother and I landed
in New Orleans, in the heat.
The city's stench nauseated us,
mosquitoes slipping through
our window screen.
At the Lake Shore Sears
he caressed lipstick
red fenders, sank fingers

in the comfort of seats.
The smallest model
was striped with silver,
and he hugged it
like a long lost niece.
In a patois of his own,
he bargained, told
universal dirty jokes.
We rode two on a nearby lawn,
sunshine, cool morning breeze.
We parked them outside
Morrison's where our waitress
said she bought all
her clothes from Sears.
That night I undressed her
gently, stroked her breasts
with my cheeks.
She sighed, and I heaved,
the air in her room
scented with my dreams.
In the morning she said
I talked in my sleep,
raved at someone,
kept asking
"What kind of flower
you want planted
next to your grave?"

Watermelon Tales

January. Snow. For days I have craved
        watermelons, wanted
    to freckle the ground with seeds,
to perform a ritual:
        Noon time, an early
    summer Sunday, the village
chief faces north, spits seven mouthfuls,
        fingers a circle
    around a galaxy of seeds.

      • • •

Maimoon the Bedouin visited in
        summer, always with
    a gift: a pick-up truck load
of watermelons. "Something for
        the children," he explained.
    Neighbors brought wheelbarrows to
fetch their share. Our chickens ate the rest.

      • • •

        His right ear pricked up
    close, my father taps on a
watermelon, strokes as though it were
        a thigh. A light slap.
    "If it doesn't sound like your hands
clapping at a wedding, it's not yours."

      • • •

        Men shake the chief's hand,
    children kiss it. Everyone files
behind him when he walks back. No one

talks until the tomb
of the local saint. The rich
place coin sacks at his feet, the poor leave
cups of melon seeds.

• • •

Maimoon also brought us meat,
gazelles he rammed with his truck.
His daughter, Selima,
said he once swerved off the road
suddenly, drove for an hour until
he spotted six. He hadn't
hit any when the truck ran out
of gas. Thirty yards away the gazelles
stood panting, and he
ran to catch one with bare hands.

• • •

Two choices, my father's doctor tells me:
transplant or six months
of pain. Outside the office,
I point to a fruit stall, the seller
waving off flies with
a feather fan. My father
strokes, slaps, and when I lift the melon
to my shoulder says
"Eleven years in America
and you carry a watermelon
like a peasant!"

• • •

Uncle Abdallah buries
a watermelon underneath the

approach of the waves—
"Like a refrigerator
down there." It's July, a picnic at
Tokara Beach. We're
kicking a ball when
my brother trips hard on the hole. He's
told to eat what he'd
broken too soon. I watched him
swallow pulp, seed, salt, and sand.

• • •

Her shadow twice her
height, the village sorceress
walks to where the chief spat. She reveals
the size of the harvest,
chance of drought, whose sons will wed
whose daughters, and names of elders whose
ailments will not cease.

• • •

Selima told the gazelle
story sitting in a tub. With soap,
my mother scrubbed the girl's scalp,
tossing handfuls of foam against
the white tile. She then
poured kerosene on Selima's
hair, rubbed till lice slid down her face,
combed till the tines
filled with the dead.

• • •

Selima married. My mother sent her
a silver anklet,

a green silk shawl, and decided
against an ivory comb. My father paid
        the sheikh to perform
    the wedding. A week later
at his door, the sheikh found three water-
        melons and a gazelle-
    skin prayer rug, a tire mark
across the spot where he would have rested his
        his head in prostration.

        • • •

    I cut the melon we bought
into cubes, strawberry red. But they were
        dry, almost bitter.
    After the third taste, my father
dropped his fork. He gazed at the window
        for a while, and spent
    the rest of the day in bed.

The Bus Driver Poem

I wasn't driving
just crossing a street
with trees, leaves mustard
yellow and ketchup red,
when a low ranking employee
of an insignificant bureaucracy
gave me the finger.
Did my face foretell
seven years of drought?
Did I remind him of
Don Kirschner, The Bee
Gees, the Cold War?
As usual I was lost
between the stuffed
tomatoes of my youth
and a future that says tick
tock boom boom.
Lost because I was living
the now of hurried afternoons,
the present that makes me bark
"No, I don't need help"
to the teenager bagging
my groceries at Mr. D's.
So when the bus driver
gave me the finger,
I gave him the Italian arm.
Brakes screeched, people inside
jerked around like carcasses
in a hot dog plant. He stepped
out shouting, big mouth

flashing. I couldn't hear
a sound. Still
I screamed fuck you,
fuck you, and the present
became a rabbit searching
for its severed head.
I mean the now was Reba
McEntire crooning to Sid
Vicious biting on a slide guitar.
Then the present burned
a heap of old calendars—
June 23, 91,
March 4, 92, the smoke
of all those days!
I didn't look back
but watched my life
from a helicopter
or a sewer hole, my heart
pounding 140 fists a minute.
Look at me, look at me
fling hours at the universe,
headbutt my old friend fear,
knee the wide skirts of hope.

The Road from Biloxi

Qadar blew at a cigarette, stuck his head
out the window. Carol wondered why she left,
was beginning to see living in peace
with the rebels that took her father's ranch.
My brother and I up front wondered why
we hadn't killed each other all these years.
We were stuck on the Biloxi highway, mid-July,
the AC kaput, and what the radio played
didn't matter, Randy Travis on the rise,
the days of disco a bruised heap, Reagan,
Meese, Jane Fonda, and the gain in the pain.
Of course, we all felt like burning American flags
on behalf of a hundred justifiable causes.
But who cares? We were stuck for hours,
stuck in 1982, and what blocked the way didn't matter,
and the sea we went to see no big deal,
a great disappointment in fact, an ocean
brow-beaten by a river, rumbling, moaning
black-eyed, bruised, weighed by Mississippi silt.
And the salty air we came to breathe
did not appear, only swamp algae
and the death smell of moss, the slime,
the invisible webs that trapped ghosts
in lukewarm water, the dead who would not dissolve.
Tom Sawyer, not dissolving, Huck Finn
not dissolving, Big Jim not dissolving,
Cherokee tears floating on top like drops of oil,
Lakotas still dreaming down, Kiowas
still coming down, Sioux still floating,
still in the Mississippi where everything seemed

tenuous, everything seemed it would revert back
to the dreams of sickly pale men and women,
back to the nightmares of runagates and domestics,
all hanging there, in the air over Biloxi,
clinging to crayfish and the gnarled hands of shrimpers.
It hovered ominous, a poisonous lethargy
not far from the town we lived in, which God knows
did not matter, making tomorrow matter even less
as long as we were here week after and the month.
Next time, we promised, it'll be the Atlantic, next time
some salty immensity, some honest to goodness breeze,
the smell of the earth turning around itself,
a clear run to the horizon, a clean shot to Africa,
to something we could beckon and understand,
something the waves would release us from
now that we were stuck here on the Biloxi road
chained, and chain smoking, aware of the sea
we left behind, and that had left us,
the Mediterranean, that other swamp, too far
to touch us again, too far to ever matter.

Echo & Elixir 1

It shines through clouds and rain.
It dyes the streets with its pink blossoms.
The day crawls through its tunnels.
The roads are long and long.

City without words. Night without night.
Somewhere I remember
these clothes are not my clothes.
These bones are not my bones.

I forget and remember again.
Ships in the harbor which is the sea
which is the journey
that awakens a light inside my chest.

Look at the hands turning the knobs.
The hands that haul the machine.
The man on the phone calling,
hanging up, calling again.

Dust and twisted nails, pebbles
and pieces of broken china,
and all the sweeping that goes on in the world.
No help.

No use saying "I will wait."

It flowers into decades of May.
It shines the windows with your passing gaze.

Echo & Elixir 3

Cigarettes in the bar, a beer,
the odyssey ends with a boarding pass.
In the duty-free shops, does one buy
perfume or Tunisian dates?
People do not ask how long you've been away,
but what have you brought?
And being away is all you bring.
Trepidation fills your shoulder bag,
and the ache writes a book of coffee
grinds and your mother's bread.

I've been reading Plato looking for a word.
Dirt reddens and browns, yellows and grays.
Abdulhamid the Scribe, Barthes, Fanon,
Abdulrahman Falcon of Quraish.
Gilgamesh still on his boat waiting
to land on beaches full of people who wait.
In your absence, there is no avoiding legend,
yet you are still a child.
Sappho and Khansa taught you that.
And the life in the hands you shake,
the poetry in the sand more than the poetry in poetry.

I am a spirit and a body.
The trees speak a language of light and thorns.
Let me tell you a story now.
You see a city in the clouds
and give it a woman's name,
always a woman's name.
Let me tell you about my loved one's hair.
You take a blade of grass
and for a second
you are a citizen of its taste.

D. H. Melhem

D. H. Melhem was born in Brooklyn, graduated from New York University, and earned her M.A. and Ph.D. from the City University of New York. She is the author of seven poetry collections, her *Notes on 94th Street* the first book of poems in English by an Arab American woman. Her writings (including poems, scholarly books, essays, novels, and a musical drama) have been honored with numerous awards, among them an American Book Award and fellowships from the National Endowment for the Humanities and the Fondation Ledig-Rowohlt in Lausanne, Switzerland. She has received unstinting praise from fellow poets, including the late Gwendolyn Brooks, who called her "serious, fervent, meticulous . . . one of the most remarkable minds of our time." Her poems create a world that is "expansive and diverse," for which Melhem "sounds a trumpet of humanity and compassion." A founding member of the International Women's Writing Guild, she serves as its vice-president.

New York Times, August 15, 1976
"As Lebanon Dies"

my background is lebanese
and peaceful, I said
proud of redundancy

grandmother beirut
grandfather damascus
my father tripoli
on the clear coast, a boy
diving for sea-urchins

now the tides cast
their dead blossoms

to sprawl at the roots of cedars
whose ancient tongues
weep fire in the sun

Broadway Music

The musicians at the newsstand
are singing
they sing and play instruments
the saxophone and cracked guitar
bawl and whine over exhaust fumes and garbage dust
they play and play   the dirty black cap open between them
on the ground—
two old men for pennies.

And a big, drunken woman laughs
laughs over her balloon stomach
she pulls up her sweater to show it
the string holding up her skirt
hanging from the big white belly
she laughs through the spaces between her teeth
her mouth looks purple and half-vacant
                    when she opens it
she shows the old men her distended belly
as if it were fruitful or cherished
she lifts her paper bag to her mouth
like a trumpet—and drinks.

She is singing now, softly, then begins
a hard hoarse cry of a note
and holds it. She is singing—

a little wine left in the bottle
the flavor that was in it
a harsh joy in the emptying

And the old men sing with her
they dream through the curving wood and metal
and the forms of the sounds that go out
as if the dirty newspapers and today's news
the people running up subway stairs
the dogs the pimps the hustlers the
gleaning-eyed girls, the howling police cars
their bullhorn commands, the litter
and dust-filtered daylight
as if these held the moment of art
as if it could be made
from the unlovely flesh, half-clay, half-dust
as if it could all be molded again, and the players
were gods empowering a new music

the big-bellied woman
and the musicians
at the newsstand

On the tendency toward solipsism in literature

1.

Where am I in your poems?
How can you be there without
the boundary defining you—the place
we are accomplishing? Are you
a blob, unmanageable endless omnivore,
a science fiction fact, the total topographical
of earth, a mobile constellation, quirky quasar,
voluminous vegetal omniscient—
how about that?
Where are you leading—except
to Parmenides, his circle
spherically flat?

2.

The unimpassioned poem is retrospective of a flight
responsible only to
its own hovering images that link
Ming vases with the tense
of made things, of mental surfaces, and with feelings
shaped to the fixed glaze of a tight, washable glisten.
Feathers can dust the unimpassioned poem
where nothing
importunately clings

but the poem whose rude textures
grapple with the live space
around the self
can grip the air
and hold light, and fly
as the earth flies

from Rest in Love

part one

There, by the rail, my mother at seventeen
pale, her thin white arm
raised, as in salute
to a seagull
trailing the ship, *Homeric,*
September, nineteen twenty-two.
Black dress flutters
behind her,
a silken whispering
about her knees covered
with black hose
above black shoes
mourning
the year-hardened mystery of her father
who disappeared en route
to a Turkish town.

Thinking of him—
of you, grandfather ever unknown to me,
your watch lying on a
hotel room nighttable
and your wallet beside it:
  a political act?

1920:
a man of Damascus, merchant, respected
having lived in peace among Turks
through the war
may have enemies

(or followed by cries of the tortured priest?
   memory of lists not destroyed—
      seized from meticulous files?)

The search, the police, the waiting,
the year with no word created your death, circumstantial,
everyone saying it then. Excepting your mother,
she who had gone to the Patriarch in Damascus
when he claimed you, singer, composer of church music,
for the clergy, and told him
a thousand devils lay under his miter.

For the ceremony of reality
throughout the house they hung
crepe on the pictures
and wreathed the door.
The priest came
and the neighbors with solemn church faces.

The old woman asked why the death knell tolled.

Struck, hope-gouged
filled with the sound
like lava pouring from the belfry to the town
burning streets   the molten windows
collapsing   until choking
she rose from her wheelchair
and the marble floors raised their surface of tombs
as she stumbled into a bathroom. Died.

Mother, historian, I question you
as the past wheels in a wakeful spray
and you speak:

Here at the rail, I am thinking of Mersine,
walking with friends in my garden of flowers
away from this ship.   Seven children
being taken to America by our mother.
Our brother there:
the first boy
after losing a son
two pairs of twins
after three living daughters
first boy
pampered and brilliant
reserved for his studies
sent early to school by my father
a prodigy
long curls like Mozart
sent to college in America
and we follow
with my father gone.

I miss my friends
the nuns at St. Joseph de l'Apparition
my flowers
the oleander
fig trees
the orange grove
everything receding
into sea foam
the wake of this ship
distantly distantly
a piano is singing
with a young man's voice

what's ahead
I don't want it, I think
but my mother
is wisdom
yet I suffer
am not strong like her
like the others
all watching
my brother,
king
strictly
encircled

my mother trusts me
because I like him
though I wonder, sometimes
why a son should be king
of his brothers and sisters

my mother is strong
and has suffered
I account
her losses . . .

Pensive girl:
it was easy to love you, miracle
fallen off a moving train when you were seven
favored thereafter among six sisters
nearly esteemed with the eldest brother
by your mother.
An achievement, in a large family,
for a girl. . . .

from Country: An Organic Poem

1.

I sing the generous dead who live with me
companionate their silence fills the still page
of my day

body is deficient   loud   metamorphic
cannot be long held

yet I praise toward our speechless act
conversations : printed

2.

George Washington : :
you have addressed me
in the resonance of your portrait
the marble statue your conscience
a vein in stone pulses
the temple your brain
columns that span rivers

Catalogue 122 : : AMERICANA with an emphasis on
California and the West. Bookmarket, Hollywood, CA.

An Eulogy on the Illustrious Life and Character of George Washington. 21 pp.
Sewn.

An Oration on the Sublime Virtues of General George Washington. Disbound.

Thoughts on the Cause of the Present Discontents. In excellent condition.

. . . .

16.

to write the country
as a poem
incomplete
is the truth
of geography

. . . .

18.

Coney Island

Over the Bridge and East River
my eyes Hart Crane and the Brooklyn span
I take the steel road to Sea Beach
the past rolling through wheels
of the N train whose new cars
speak no and never
to old vehicles junkyarded
in memory

Beholding the Stillwell Avenue Station
from elevated tracks
I descend the desolate ramp
jostled by ghost-crowds
their bathing bags and picnic lunches
their smell of coffee and expectations
they walk they walk with me
my hand in my mother's
to see Coney Island
to ride the Ferris Wheel
eat at Nathan's

We will swim in the ocean
thrashing a small space
for ourselves

But
having taken the N train
I go down the ramp alone
my hand extended to you O Sorrow
to you O happy invention
and there through the gates
at the foot of incline
on the streets of ice cream
the way of delight
is closed   the Tornado
is closed   I run to the Boardwalk—
door to a childhood of 31 Rides
Steeplechase The Funny Place
boarded up   Kiddie Ride
churns empty cars
toward the sea
pinched by jetties

I step down to the salt edge
with birdcries dredged from clearing water

What is retrieved?

Gulls paddling like ducks
in a pool hewn by rain
clouds opening a fan
across the sun
clouds bunching like sheep
to the right

arrows to the left

What is retrieved?

Reader/Adviser Speaks
Seven Languages   Babel tongues
the starry stripes
flap with the flag
of the Polar Bear Club

Yearlong bathers
share winter sun
on a concrete slab

A tough leans over
the Boardwalk railing
aims at naked feet
and spits

I walk on
to the subway
chilled

. . . .

20.

Culture is not the self, not a confection
gobbled anonymous at
a cotton candy seashore

On the boardwalk I paint you in the contours
of your colors
Write me a poem as I render your image
tell me yourself, our tangents and integrations

with reverent ear let us listen into a shell
for breakers   and the dangerous sun

· · · · · · · ·

54.

And still the dream leans over parapet
toward a river of elusive fish,
the blue-hatted woman with a book,
dogs ambling grassward in sunlight.
Mind comes to rest in its images,
enjoying them one by one from a vista
over apple tree with apples
above reach, by a plane tree
turning wild. Wilderness crouches
on high branches, in thickets, glides
at evening along riverbank, grows inward.
On a summer Sunday I leave the scene, enter
the air-conditioned supermarket, buy
an onion, apples, bread, and canned sardines. . . .

September 11, 2001, World Trade Center, Aftermath

1.

Under a hard blue sky
a white shroud rises.

Uptown
air turns acrid.
I close my windows.

Cloud messages
from the plume of hell,
I breathe you, taste the mist—
concrete dust, chairs, shoes,
files, photos, handbags, rings, a doll,
upholstery, breakfast trays,
body parts and parting words
and screams.

Blood of workers, passengers, police—
O firemen running up stairs
past people streaming
from a tower poised to crash—

I breathe you flowing
into the ceaseless sacrifice
of innocents.

My TV exhales frantic images:

Have you seen her? Have you seen him?
Everybody loved her. He was my friend.
Anybody seen them?

Anger rolls over grief and prayers.
"Vengeance!" echoes from toxic caves.

Like spores of a giant fungus,
rage races through the air.
"Vengeance!" the people cry.
All die again.

2.
Union Square Park, Two Weeks Later:
A Pilgrimage

Sunday,
a day as sunny as that other.
Slowly, beneath the trees,
along wire fences garlanding the grass
with flowers, candles, prayers,
love messages on colored papers, photographs,
I walk with vigilant mourners winding past.

Level with branches, George Washington,
astride a horse, carries a fireman's flag
and a peace flag tipped red with a Valentine heart:
"One people."
Invocations anoint his pedestal:
"Love One Another, Give Peace a Chance."

Seated before him on the ground,
Buddhists in unison strike their prayer drums.
Nearby, a couple collect for the Firemen's Fund.
Across the park, pipers and drummers
march past Abraham Lincoln,
proclaim "The Battle Hymn of the Republic."

Later, in a drugstore stocked with filter masks
I buy a box. Each one disclaims protection
from toxic dust and poison gas.

Drawn to my City's visible wound
I go downtown.
The subway's nearly empty. I climb
into streets without traffic, buildings powdered white.
Tourists and residents aim their cameras.

On Fulton Street
I join the pilgrimage downhill.

Mask ready, I taste the faintest breath
of acrid smoke, invisible incense
of cries and clamor
still peopling the air.
A woman pulls a suitcase,
a man pulls his.
Which one returns to a ghost apartment,
which one flees?

I reach the crowd and Broadway barricades.
Girders, twisted and wrenched into a pile,
lie helpless beside a jagged crater.
Distant survivor buildings at the rim
face the great square of chaos
a sixteen-acre graveyard. Earth
must have birthed canyons like this,
quaking tectonic rage.

A yellow crane poises high
in homage to the standing shell—

that spire, that Coliseum,
Tower of Pisa leaning grief
against a phantom Twin.

Ground Zero, ground of martyrs, crushed and burned,
their screaming blood bones ashes pulverized
into cement clouds wind carries
through the city to the world.
The crowd, in hushed and rumbling awe,
slows down to get a better view.
"Keep moving!" a bullhorn shouts.

Into the roiling space
an old sign on a building calls:
A GOOD TIME TO INVEST!

A policeman who had been there from the first
explains to a visitor why people jumped from windows,
those whom a child had witnessed
as birds afire. I wonder if
they'd wildly hoped for flight.

We speak of gratitude.
"I feel the love," he says.

The air falls heavier.
I press a mask against my nose.
My eyes smart a little.
I pass the glass façade of an empty store.
On pedestals, new shoes
display their dust.
A lone pub signals with a scrawl,
"We're Open!"

My skin begins to hurt.
I need to find a subway,
take home
my heartload.

The train shuns regular stops.
At 96th Street
I find a trash can,
throw the mask away.

Epilogue, Earth Speaks

You blast omnivorous graves
where millions in memory lie,
you foul my pleasant air,
you level my mountains of ore.

With greed your guiding law,
and vengeance as your creed,
your justice is suspect,
your mercy is select.
All life deserves respect.

Confront the suffering
you mutually inflict.
Share your crusts of bread—
loaves will multiply.
Staunch my terrible wounds
and heal your own thereby.

Let barren hearts accept
seeds from compassionate rain.

Love is the sternest prayer.
All life deserves respect.

Philip Metres

Poet and translator Philip Metres was born in 1970 in San Diego. He graduated from Holy Cross College and earned both an M.F.A. and a Ph.D. from Indiana University. He writes "subtle, accomplished, shimmering poems that explore the nuances of being an outsider in a language." He is the author of two poetry chapbooks, *Instants* and *Primer for Non-Native Speakers*, from which a selection was included in the *Best American Poetry* series, and a full-length collection, *To See the Earth*. Metres has also translated two collections, *Catalogue of Comedic Novelties: Selected Poems of Lev Rubinstein* and *A Kindred Orphanhood: Selected Poems of Sergey Gandlevsky*, and *Behind the Lines: War Resistance Poetry on the Armenian Homefront since 1945*. A recipient of fellowships from the Thomas J. Watson Foundation, the National Endowment for the Arts, Ledig House, and the Ohio Arts Council, Metres teaches literature and creative writing at John Carroll University in Cleveland, Ohio. Were it not for Ellis Island, his last name would be Abourjaili.

One more story   he said   In a restaurant in Amsterdam

a young woman   came in
speaking Arabic   I said you are Iraqi
she said I haven't eaten for three days
I said what do you mean   she said
I need to turn   turn myself in
this was a strange language to me
a different logic   Come and sit I said
food brought out   she ate   finally
spoke   her husband now in Istanbul
they'd escaped Iraq   he was taxi driver
sold his car paid $5,000 to Turkish driver
to send her   Istanbul to Amsterdam
a big truck   crates of fruit and vegetables
had a tiny space   in the middle   kept her

there gave her food and water supposed to last
seven days   lasted four strange language
mouth of the truck   she was stuck
in one position for seven days   could not
move crates of figs   pallets cracked
blocked   lodged   then they just dropped her
in the middle of Amsterdam right then   she was
hoping waiting   turn myself in   my husband not
far behind   strange language to me   I did not
understand   turn myself in   in the middle
of Amsterdam do you speak   speak

Ashberries: Letters

1.

Outside, in a country with no word
for *outside*, they cluster on trees,

red bunches. I looked up
ryabina, found *mountain ash*. No

mountains here, just these berries
cradled in yellow leaves.

When I rise, you fall asleep. *We
barely know each other*, you said

on the phone last night. Today, sun brushes
the wall like an empty canvas, voices

from outside drift into this room. I can't
translate—my words, frostbitten

fingers. I tell no one, how your hands
ghost over my back, letters I hold.

2.

Reading children's stories by Tolstoy,
Alyosha traces his index

over the alphabet his mouth so easily
unlocks. Every happy word resembles

every other, every unhappy word's
unhappy in its own way. Like apartments

at dusk. Having taken a different street
from the station, I was lost in minutes.

How to say, where's the street like this,
not this? Keys I'd cut for years coaxed open

no pursed lips. How to say, blind terror?
Sprint, lungburn, useless tongue? How say

thank you, muscular Soviet worker, fading
on billboard, for pointing me the way?

3.

Alyosha and I climbed trees to pick berries, leaves
almost as red. On ladders, we scattered

half on ground, playing who could get them
down the other's shirt without their knowing.

Morning, the family gone, I ground the berries
to skin, sugared sour juices twice.

Even in tea they burned. In the yard,
leafpiles of fire. Cigarettes between teeth,

the old *dvorniks* rake, scratch the earth,
try to rid it of some persistent itch.

I turn the dial, it drags my finger back.
When the phone at last connects to you, I hear

only my own voice, crackle of the line.
The rakes scratch. Flames hiss and tower.

4.

This morning, the trees bare. Ashberries
on long black branches. Winter. My teacher

says they sweeten with frost, each snow
a sugar. Each day's dark grows darker,

and streets go still, widen, like ice over lakes,
and words come slow to every chapped mouth,

not just my own, having downed a little vodka
and then some tea. Tomorrow I'll bend down

branches, brittle with cold, pluck what I can't
yet name, then jar the pulp and save the stones.

What to say? Love, I live for the letters
I must wait to open. They bear across

this land, where I find myself at a loss—
each word a wintering seed.

A House Without

—for Lily Boulos

1. Portrait of Lily in Front of 290 Hicks Street

Homely brownstone. Black hair, seventy years
ungrayed. Arches of eyebrows and aisles,

stained glass gaze and minaret mind. You take
everyone in, and raise them. Your hand always

cold, grow thick in the knuckles, numb
to dishes from the oven. How did they feel

tender on my nape? Your faux pearls
and rosaries, sayings and saints and dark

household God. Who could ever believe
they know you? You swallow your mother tongue.

One by one we abandon the rooms, and leave
a button you like: "Just visiting this planet."

You always dished out more than we could chew.
Now you feed the soil. What house is left without you?

2. Housework

All day she'd work but things didn't
stay clean. When we came to stay,

my father shuddered at the sight
of her knees, tattooed by the floor

of the dim rooms she scrubbed. After the war,
why did his father come home

to another woman first and not his mother?
In the book she loved and left me,

The Potato Eaters sit and eat, just one lantern
to light innumerable browns: dun, earth,

smoke, and peasant eyes. I want to see
in the dark her mystic disdain

for light, a still life of Depression shelves
brimming with chipped tea cups, lampshades and twine.

3. Making Meshi

I was five, rolling grape leaves
into thick fingers: *meshi. Ne touche pas,
ne touche pas*, my father trying to hug

his mother's back, proudly bowed
before the oven. *God-damned French
hudda.* Everyone laughed

when Grandpa swore in Arabic, as if
the language itself were a punch line.
Plucking grape leaves from

the patio vine. Everyone reaching
for words to describe them, all garlic
lemon on the tongue. Why did he talk

to her like that? Washing,
spreading the leaves open,
veins pointed up. Grandma's tongue

a Beirut convent, Grandpa's tongue
planted between his teeth, biting off
his Arabic. It was pride,

the way they held
or lashed their tongues. Spooning spiced rice
into the palm. Folding the base

inward to center. Grandpa scolded a cusser:
what kind of language is that? Aroma
of arms. Tucking the wings in

—but unwinding, undone in young fingers.
I can't keep them all together. Laying torn leaves
to blanket the pot. Years later, lying in

my father's room, in summer's
oven, I heard them, whispering, in their bed. Beyond
the wall, all embers and breathing.

4. *Ascent*

She leans against the stairwell railing,
trying to catch her breath

as if it were a moth, hovering
around a bulb, just out of reach. Her heart

failing for months now, her lungs exhausted
as night swimmers, arms flailing

the black glass of water for something solid.
The knifepoint of each inhaling.

In the convent, as a teen, she could steal
the ball from any priest and swish a shot

from thirty feet. Now, in her last ascent,
she turns, looks down the unmirroring well

and grabs the rail as if it were an arm
of someone trying to rob her.

5. The Landing

Grapevines snake through broken
      panes. Stairs now quiet, reek
          of acrid mold, fallen

plaster. Water pipes burst
      twice since her lungs flooded,
          the sump of her heart stalled.

When something was lost, she'd pray
      to St. Anthony, who'd lived
          his last days in the arms

of a tree, descending only
      to eat. Then, a sudden thirst
          for the dust of the city

of his birth. He walked till he could see
      the gates. Then he was carried.

6. The Attic Bird

Where the staircase ends, where I sleep
when all the beds are full. Where Salma wakes
each day to the Statue of Liberty. In 1950,

age eighteen, she arrives, a seamstress
who resides in the gorgeous weave
of Arabic alone—each letter a painting

of what could not be painted. Salma,
the last of her family, will never marry.
Her parents disown her when she hangs the cat

who ate the family chickens. Attic bird
that my grandmother-cowbird dupes
to roost above her brood, Salma grieves

like a widow when the one she raises,
marries and moves away. Her red hair
shocks to white. Her eyes widen. Her face

retreats to the necklace of bones. When no one's left,
her "son" returns to take her back
to Lebanon, where a convent will nurse her to God.

The radiator clings, as if Lily were in the kitchen
still banging out her own Morse Code,
calling Salma down for the phone.

7. House Cleaning

We spend all day dismantling the years
floor by floor, now toss and turn
in unfamiliar walls, trying to remember
a faded oriental rug, the edges worn
ragged, soggy from the floods, a table
lacquered black and black and gouged by mistake,
a powder blue statuette of Mary
grinding her holy heel on a snake,

Baltimore Catechism and *Vanity Fair,*
Paris Match and *The Cloud of Unknowing,*
Lust for Life and *Lady Chatterley's Lover*—
the musty walls of books Lily dreamed in—
the whole housewide Brooklyn dumpster
picked clean, that night, while we sleep.

8. *Inheritance*

Out on our porch, out facing the shapeless
dark of moonless night, my father told us
how, his mother still unconscious, he rose
from his childhood bed, the room cluttered
with what he'd always seen as junk, trinkets
his mother hoarded and stirred
to life with prayer to saints she figured
bodily, and good on their promises:
Saint Jude, patron of desperate cases.
Saint Anthony, patron of the lost. Eyes

closed, he could walk each room of the house
in his mind. At the hospital, he found her
sitting up, in a white hospital gown,
still-black hair combed to small shoulders,
looking calmly out the far window, at dawn,
and at that moment knew she would die
and he would live on. And that he would live
only in light of her living. He shifted his eyes
to us, as if someday we would save him.

9. Memory Jar

Qui se ressemble, s'assemble.
Invitation is the sincerest form
of fluttering. Lily, it's dark
and I can't see you. *La patience*
est un virtue. Cliché, a cocktail dress
you wore to hide your shy desire:
five months pregnant with my father,
you had no idea why you tired
climbing stairs. *When you work,*
you have one demon; without work,
you face a thousand. The dark house
even dark in day. The house in pieces.
A thousand nights torment the lazy
golden silence. My hands grope the walls
in a dark foyer. A house without
children runs away from you. *Qui s'excuse,*
s'accuse. In case of emergency, contact
someone you've never known. I ask
and ask. *Qui ne dit mot, consent.*
When you run after a woman, she runs away
like a house without windows. When you
leave, she pursues you.

Haas H. Mroue

A graduate of the University of California–Los Angeles Film School and the University of Colorado, Haas H. Mroue authored or coauthored over twenty-five travel guidebooks. His poetry collection about the Lebanese civil war, *Beirut Seizures*, "is a powerful and artful response to a historical moment marked by elusiveness and pain." With their "noun-centered syntax and a coded austerity of effect," his poems redefine the lyric style and create an "esthetics of distance." Until his untimely death in 2007, he divided his time between Washington State and London.

Beirut Survivors Anonymous

My generation was lost. Cities
too. And nations.
                    —Czeslaw Milosz

In Beirut on good
nights I watch rockets fly
over rooftops until my eyes hurt.
I listen for names of the dead
on the radio, putting faces to names,
scars to bodies, burns to flesh.
I remove my contacts by candlelight
and flush my eyes with Dettol.

Years later, now
I pick up the telephone
needing to call someone who remembers.
I have always been alone. But now I sink
and it's not the Mediterranean.
I fly coach cross-continent
searching for someone

to recreate my childhood with.
We are walking to school. It is May.
It is sixteen years ago. Strawberries
piled high on carts explode. Bits of cars
and shrapnel and glass melt
on our skin. I help the strawberry
vendors pick strawberries
from the gutter. Later, my mother
spreads yogurt on my burns.

We lived a war with no name
and escaped. We now belong to a culture
that has no name.
My generation drives BMWs
down streets in Los Angeles or Long Island
popping ecstasy pills hoping to be artistic,
chanting for Hare Hare Krishna on the corner
of College and 13th, wishing for a flying roadblock,
Howitzers, snipers, anything
to replace the monotony of oceans
for the rhythm of the Mediterranean.

It is for nights of unrelenting shelling
we long, for the calm of corridors and neighbors
boiling coffee until dawn, for gunpowder seeping
through shut windows and the wails
of a single ambulance.

We drink *arak* in Oriental restaurants
in Denver or Burbank or Fort Lauderdale.
We watch belly-dancers and vomit hummous
with no garlic, hummous as thick as coffee
at the AUB milkbar. We live in a daze

longing for green plums and salt,
the ecstasy of Howitzers on a school night.

You can look in our eyes
and see we've been to Beirut. We are not amiable
to snipers unless they are aiming at us. Our eyes
change color in the dark, the dark of basements,
corridors and bathrooms with no windows.
We are experiencing post-traumatic stress
somewhere in Massachusetts, Colorado.
We don't attend Beirut Survivors Anonymous.
We still smell the gunpowder and salty cheese
bubbling on pastry for breakfast.
We can still hear the wind hissing
after a car-bomb.

We are the remains of a Howitzer,
a 155, of Merkavas and T-72s
and soldiers at checkpoints who steal
our Ray-Bans. We are young
and need to shield our eyes.

Arabes Despatriados

1.

No one believes me when I say
my ancestors found America.
Phoenicians in wooden boats
sailed the Mediterranean past Carthage
and Marseille, the Canary Islands
and weeks on rough waters
to America.

They had olive skin, dark hair,
one eyebrow. They could read
and write. They traded with Israelites,
Assyrians, and when they landed
on the new continent did not cry out
India!

They did not run back for gold
or black men. They had the alphabet.
They had no use for chains.
After years of sailing they always went home
to Saida, Tyre, Byblos or Sarafand
hilly cities facing the sea, facing west,
where they built houses and pressed olives.

2.

My ancestors built Granada
carved water canals in the earth
to feed the orange trees of Andalusia.
When I stand on top of a mountain
at Orgiva, Granada at my feet,

water from Esekiahs trickling
down hillsides, I suck on a sweet fig
and imagine my grandfathers planting fig trees
before they discovered the New World
before they were labeled Hungaros,
Arabes Despatriados,
terrorists.

3.

My grandfather's house in Saida
faced the sea. He too sailed
the Mediterranean past Gibraltar
and the Azores
to America.

In Hermosillo he found Carmen
her skin as smooth as the sea
on August nights. When war broke out
he traveled north to California
to buy and sell. He grew a mustache
and grew tired of trains and the dust
clinging to his boots. He sailed
back home to Saida alone
and never loved again.

4.

In California, in the midst
of drought-ridden summers
I can feel my grandfather's longing
for the crashing of waves,
the salt on Carmen's skin,
the dust of Baja, a shot of Tequila

and the smell of his textile factory
in Hermosillo.

And when I stand on top of a hill
at Skyros, Latchi or Antibes
and look east I can see my ancestors
sailing the Mediterranean, heading east
heading home
away from rough Atlantic waters
away from the people who would later
call them Hungaros, Arabes Despatriados,
terrorists.

Civil War

In a country of many sects
and fig trees
I walk the streets alone.

I call out to you across the Green Line:
Ignore the war and it will devour you.

Give me back my testicles
my sister's nipples
my cherry tree.

I spray graffiti on abandoned walls.
We are coyotes
rabbits
fleas.

On a balcony of a bombed out skyscraper
I dangle my soul out for you.
Snipers, where are you?
Don't ignore me now.

On a minaret I shout into a loudspeaker
I do not belong to you.
Over a church bell I scream
I do not belong to you.

I walk the streets and pity myself.
I scrape my eyes out with the cross,
collect my gushing blood
on the pages of the Koran.

I do not have any fig trees.

Adele Ne Jame

Adele Ne Jame is the author of two poetry books, *Inheritance* and *Field Work,* which was described as "the work of a truly original voice: a one-of-a-kind wonder." Her Arab heritage, and her adult life lived in French Polynesia and the islands of the South Seas, give her poetry "its rich ambiance and evocative landscape." Her poems have appeared in such journals as *Ploughshares* and the *Denver Quarterly,* and she is the recipient of a fellowship from the National Endowment for the Arts and a former poet-in-residence at the University of Wisconsin–Madison. Born in New Jersey, Ne Jame has lived since 1969 in Hawaii, where she teaches creative writing at Hawaii Pacific University.

Fieldwork, Devil's Lake, Wisconsin

This far north even an early spring
seems insufficient, though starlings
congregate overhead in the branches
and the trees are beginning their work,
though geese, beautiful in their loud
honking, fly in patterns, synchronized,
unpredictable, some wild announcement
you think must have something
to do with mending or perhaps
forgetting that the urgent wind,
like death, dismantles everything,
that even its vibrato which resonates
long in the body is evidence of a diminishing
presence, that love fails. Yet,
I am willing, though arrival seems more
like progressive loss, to attend to this
work of belief, even as a small

creature in the distance breathes evenly,
beautifully in a field of dying fire trees
finding bloodroot, its single pale flower,
willing to say after a long, unforgiving
winter that the sunlight blanching
the lake, after an overnight thaw its current
rushing with the wind's force,
is not just a matter of physics or a metaphor
gone wrong like love's hard turn back,
that in this now perfect light,
the bluffs that circle the lake
are the color of rose quartz,
that this wall of flesh,
in its own time, is equal to
the harsh grace of this landscape,
and that the loud clattering of birds
starting up again is no accident.

Annabelle's

From Bakersfield, he says,
all red in the face, sloshed, a football coach
pushing that beer gut around
      like it was the prettiest part of his body.
But the lights are twirling
round and round
making everything romantic, and he thinks

she's terrific. He takes the drink out of her hand, cinches
her waist with his heavy arm and they're gliding
across the dance floor, that two-ton Galento moving

so smooth, and he's talking and twirling her
around and through the crowd just like
he owns that floor. And she's trying
to keep up because he likes her and people
are looking and she likes it
once she gets used to it.

He lets her go some, then pulls her in
real close for more turns. But he keeps on
talking and confusing her. She's thinking
about the small of her back where his hand is
pressing so she can follow,
and she's not interested in talking at all.
But he is. So he slows down
real slow

leans back to look at her—
God, you're a beauty, he says.
Men kill themselves for a woman like you,

they do. Every day. Bust their asses
so they can give a woman like you
everything you could want. You know?
And he's messing it all up, she thinks,
sounding less drunk—everything, he says.
God, look at you. Men go nuts

over a woman like you. Work themselves
into the fucking ground, work
their asses off to give you everything, you know.
And he leans back again looking and says,
You know?
I know it by heart, she says.
And he stops, his arms gently holding her there—
What's that mean, he says.
Nothing, she says.
What'd you mean, tell me, he says.
I've been married, she says.

And he pulls her in real close again
like the whole world was his body.
You're such a pretty one, he says, twirling her

around and around. I'd marry you tonight, I would.
I'd work my ass off for you.
God, look at you. I'd give you everything,
everything you could want.

A Blessing (for my daughter)

Silence was Thoreau's proof against cynicism.
William Bronk

Outside your window the morning air is a whirl
of blossoms and rain as if working furiously
towards some gladness—, and you asleep
as I watch, working out some dream
of your life—now where it is all a beginning,
paused like a diver on the high board, balancing
all her weight on her toes, heart like a furnace
that moment before the fall into the unforgettable blue.

And what counter statement can survive
the body's frenetic demands? At your waking
I might say, the moon comes and goes—,
or mention the black angel whose wings are velvet
and always widespread—, or offer instead
the story of my father's sister, eighty years ago
a child herself, who after losing
ten brothers and sisters to the great war,
walked across the blazing desert alone
from Damascus to Beirut. Her whirling robes
like her heart, a weapon against that ruined world.

But on a morning like this when the light
gathers around you with inexpressible
grace and privacy,
the words seem somehow indecorous—,
so I offer instead an unspoken blessing,
the heart's caesura, and yield again
to love's last work, its silent implosion.

A Love Story

Samuel's eyes were round and dark,
and his smile like a kid's no matter
how fast he got old. He married
Esther, a Lebanese girl from Havana.
She was perfect and he loved her.
Her wavy hair in the photo spread over
her bare shoulders, her beautiful eyes were
like powerful horses running hard over flat land.
Samuel called her einey,
Arabic for my eyes, meaning
dearer than vision. But after a son
and years, she stopped loving him.
Absolutely like death.
She went back to Havana and Samuel
began his second life.
He treasured the suffering.
Kept sheep's blood
in a jar on the counter.
Walked the streets
at night with a love that would not yield.
For years flew the night shuttle
to Havana, arms full of gifts.
He never gave it up.
Even when they found him in the fetal position,
the TV still on, they had to,
my brother said weeping over the phone,
break his legs to get him inside his coffin.

Naomi Shihab Nye

"In the current literary scene," the late William Stafford wrote, "one of the most heartening influences is the work of Naomi Shihab Nye." Nye lives in San Antonio with her husband, photographer Michael Nye, and their son. Her books include *You & Yours, Going Going, A Maze Me, 19 Varieties of Gazelle: Poems of the Middle East* (a National Book Award finalist), *Come with Me: Poems for a Journey, Fuel, Red Suitcase,* and *Habibi,* a novel for teens that won six "best book" awards. Nye's picture books include *Sitti's Secrets* and *Baby Radar.* She has edited seven anthologies of poetry for young readers, including *This Same Sky, The Tree Is Older than You Are, The Space between Our Footsteps: Poems & Paintings from the Middle East, What Have You Lost?* and *Salting the Ocean.* A visiting writer all over the world for many years, she has been a Lannan Fellow, a Guggenheim Fellow, and a Library of Congress Witter Bynner Fellow.

Different Ways to Pray

There was the method of kneeling,
a fine method, if you lived in a country
where stones were smooth.
The women dreamed wistfully of bleached courtyards,
hidden corners where knee fit rock.
Their prayers were weathered rib bones,
small calcium words uttered in sequence,
as if this shedding of syllables could somehow
fuse them to the sky.

There were the men who had been shepherds so long
they walked like sheep.
Under the olive trees, they raised their arms—
Hear us! We have pain on earth!

We have so much pain there is no place to store it!
But the olives bobbed peacefully
in fragrant buckets of vinegar and thyme.
At night the men ate heartily, flat bread and white cheese,
and were happy in spite of the pain,
because there was also happiness.

Some prized the pilgrimage,
wrapping themselves in new white linen
to ride buses across miles of vacant sand.
When they arrived at Mecca
they would circle the holy places,
on foot, many times,
they would bend to kiss the earth
and return, their lean faces housing mystery.

While for certain cousins and grandmothers
the pilgrimage occurred daily,
lugging water from the spring
or balancing the baskets of grapes.
These were the ones present at births,
humming quietly to perspiring mothers.
The ones stitching intricate needlework into children's dresses,
forgetting how easily children soil clothes.

There were those who didn't care about praying.
The young ones. The ones who had been to America.
They told the old ones, you are wasting your time.
        Time?—The old ones prayed for the young ones.
They prayed for Allah to mend their brains,
for the twig, the round moon,
to speak suddenly in a commanding tone.

And occasionally there would be one
who did none of this,
the old man Fowzi, for example, Fowzi the fool,
who beat everyone at dominoes,
insisted he spoke with God as he spoke with goats,
and was famous for his laugh.

The Art of Disappearing

When they say Don't I know you?
say no.

When they invite you to the party
remember what parties are like
before answering.
Someone telling you in a loud voice
they once wrote a poem.
Greasy sausage balls on a paper plate.
Then reply.

If they say We should get together
say why?

It's not that you don't love them anymore.
You're trying to remember something
too important to forget.
Trees. The monastery bell at twilight.
Tell them you have a new project.
It will never be finished.

When someone recognizes you in a grocery store
nod briefly and become a cabbage.
When someone you haven't seen in ten years
appears at the door,
don't start singing him all your new songs.
You will never catch up.

Walk around feeling like a leaf.
Know you could tumble any second.
Then decide what to do with your time.

Famous

The river is famous to the fish.

The loud voice is famous to silence,
which knew it would inherit the earth
before anybody said so.

The cat sleeping on the fence is famous to the birds
watching him from the birdhouse.

The tear is famous, briefly, to the cheek.

The idea you carry close to your bosom
is famous to your bosom.

The boot is famous to the earth,
more famous than the dress shoe,
which is famous only to floors.

The bent photograph is famous to the one who carries it
and not at all famous to the one who is pictured.

I want to be famous to shuffling men
who smile while crossing streets,
sticky children in grocery lines,
famous as the one who smiled back.

I want to be famous in the way a pulley is famous,
or a buttonhole, not because it did anything spectacular,
but because it never forgot what it could do.

Breaking My Favorite Bowl

Some afternoons
thud unexpectedly
and split into four pieces
on the floor.

Two large pieces, two small ones.
I could glue them back,
but what would I use them for?

Forgive me when I answer you
in a voice so swollen
it won't fit your ears.

I'm thinking about apples and histories,
the hands I broke off
my mother's praying statue
when I was four—
how she tearfully repaired them,
but the hairline cracks
in the wrists
were all she said
she could see—

the unannounced blur
of something passing
out of a life.

Blood

"A true Arab knows how to catch a fly in his hands,"
my father would say. And he'd prove it,
cupping the buzzer instantly
while the host with the swatter stared.

In the spring our palms peeled.
True Arabs believed watermelon could heal fifty ways.
I changed these to fit the occasion.

Years before, a girl knocked,
wanted to see the Arab.
I said we didn't have one.
After that, my father told me who he was,
"Shihab"—"shooting star"—
a good name, borrowed from the sky.
Once I said, "When we die, we give it back?"
He said that's what a true Arab would say.

Today the headlines clot in my blood.
A little Palestinian dangles a toy truck on the front page.
Homeless fig, this tragedy with a terrible root
is too big for us. What flag can we wave?
I wave the flag of stone and seed,
table mat stitched in blue.

I call my father, we talk around the news.
It is too much for him,
neither of his two languages can reach it.
I drive into the country to find sheep, cows,
to plead with the air:
Who calls anyone *civilized*?
Where can the crying heart graze?
What does a true Arab do now?

The Small Vases from Hebron

Tip their mouths open to the sky.
Turquoise, amber,
the deep green with fluted handle,
pitcher the size of two thumbs,
tiny lip and graceful waist.

Here we place the smallest flower
which could have lived invisibly
in loose soil beside the road,
sprig of succulent rosemary,
bowing mint.

They grow deeper in the center of the table.

Here we entrust the small life,
thread, fragment, breath.
And it bends. It waits all day.
As the bread cools and the children
open their gray copybooks
to shape the letter that looks like
a chimney rising out of a house.

And what do the headlines say?

Nothing of the smaller petal
perfectly arranged inside the larger petal
or the way tinted glass filters light.
Men and boys, praying when they died,
fall out of their skins.
The whole alphabet of living,
heads and tails of words,

sentences, the way they said,
"Ya' Allah!" when astonished,
or "ya'ani" for "I mean"—
a crushed glass under the feet
still shines.
But the child of Hebron sleeps
with the thud of her brothers falling
and the long sorrow of the color red.

What Brings Us Out

Something about pumpkins caused
the man who had not spoken in three years
to lean forward, cough, open his mouth.
How the room heaved into silence,
his words enormous in that air:
"I won't . . . be . . . afraid . . .
of my . . . father . . . anymore."
And what silence followed,
as if each heart had spoken
its most secret terror,
had combed the tangled clump
for the hardest line
and pulled it, intact,
from the mass.

I bless that man forever
for his courage, his voice
which started with one thing
and went to many, opening up and up
to the rim of the world.
So much silence had given him

a wisdom which held us all at bay,
amazed. Sometimes when I see
mountains of pumpkins by the roadside,
or watermelons, a hill of autumn gourds
piled lavishly on crates, I think
perhaps this one, or that, were it to
strike someone right,
this curl of hardened stalk,
this pleated skin . . .
or on an old bureau drawer,
the vegetable-like roundness of a glass knob
that the baby turns and turns
emerging, later, from a complicated dream . . .
the huge navigational face of a radio
which never worked while I was alive
but gave me more to go on than most sounds:
how what brings us out may be
small as that black arrow, swinging
the wide arc, the numbers where silent voices lived,
how fast you had to turn to make it move.

Jerusalem

Let's be the same wound if we must bleed.
Let's fight side by side, even if the enemy
is ourselves: I am yours, you are mine.

—Tommy Olofsson, Sweden

I'm not interested in
who suffered the most.
I'm interested in
people getting over it.

Once when my father was a boy
a stone hit him on the head.
Hair would never grow there.
Our fingers found the tender spot
and its riddle: the boy who has fallen
stands up. A bucket of pears
in his mother's doorway welcomes him home.
The pears are not crying.
Later his friend who threw the stone
says he was aiming at a bird.
And my father starts growing wings.

Each carries a tender spot:
something our lives forgot to give us.
A man builds a house and says,
"I am native now."
A woman speaks to a tree in place
of her son. And olives come.
A child's poem says,
"I don't like wars,

they end up with monuments."
He's painting a bird with wings
wide enough to cover two roofs at once.

Why are we so monumentally slow?
Soldiers stalk a pharmacy:
big guns, little pills.

If you tilt your head just slightly
it's ridiculous.

There's a place in my brain
where hate won't grow.
I touch its riddle: wind, and seeds.
Something pokes us as we sleep.

It's late but everything comes next.

Gregory Orfalea

Gregory Orfalea is the author of *The Arab Americans: A History* and several other books, including two poetry collections. "Difficult, playful, seeming to move at times to the very edge of speech," his poems "escape the silence of history." Orfalea is also coeditor of the groundbreaking anthology *Grape Leaves: A Century of Arab American Poetry.* Director of the Center for Writing at Pitzer College in Claremont, California, and professor of creative writing, he has served as a judge for the American PEN Award in Research Nonfiction. He and his wife have three sons, and he currently divides his time between Claremont and Washington, D.C.

War

And so it begins in play
with the splashing in a small pool
and the shriek at errant water
in the eye, or legs swelling
with adrenalin to run and leap.
Soon they are in a heap. And the elder
pushes the younger who has the audacity
to be there. He stares at first deeply
before crying at his brother as if
for the first time. They were one
breath of air, and now two. It is
not long before the elder has a scar
to show he is not the only one wrong.
The day and night join—see the red
pulled like seared flesh far off?
They run. They laugh and grow
and destroy. I can't stop it.
I know what happens to boys.

The Bomb That Fell on Abdu's Farm

The Phantoms approached, we were told,
    like warps in the sky, like gossip
        gone real, aimed in steel
            at the eyes of the village.

All the farmers and farmers' boys ran
    to the rooftops and watched,
        for it was terrifying
            and beautiful to see a wedge
                of silver up from the South.

And they began to fall with a
    vengeance, under the anti-air-
        craft that ringed Damascus and the
            villagers whooped for there seemed
                a magic field around their fields.

Until a cow-shed flew in red to the sky.
    And a mother milking collapsed
        in her milk. The milk ran pink.

Next door, in my great-uncle's newly-
    irrigated fields, a bomb fell.
        The mud smothered it. The mud
            talked to it. The mud wrapped
                its death like a mother. And
                    the bomb with American lettering
                    did not go off.

Water your gardens always. Always.

The Spider

Once, rain-touched,
without woman, family
or friend, in a country
too caught in the middle
to resist pain
I was pulled into the circles
of a willow backlit
by a streetlamp. Rain-
water glistened like glucose
down the black-veined bark,
whips of branches spiraling round
as if the willow had spun
out of the ground. Silent,
clear, a pearl hung
and beckoned—in.
Was the light
the spider, or I?

Once, I was lonely as death
but lifted my head in the web.

On the One in the Crook of My Chest

By chance, or nuzzling fit, this boy
has settled in the Fertile Crescent
that begins at the nub of my chin
and ends in the lap, that beginning.

And for a few moments, the front of my rib cage
and the back of his ribs fit perfectly,
bone slatting into bone,
fine Venetian blinds, comb on comb.

Is it too possessing to whisper
"My boy, " when he fills this gap
I once believed was my body?

Kevin Gerard Rashid

Lyrical and narrative, Kevin Gerard Rashid's poems possess an honesty that gives them their hard edge. Often sparked by humor and Rashid's insistence on looking past the obvious, the subjects and themes of his poems reveal the unexpected and more than what was bargained for. His poems have appeared in many journals and anthologies, including *The Academy of American Poets New Voices 1989–1990* and *Arab Detroit: From Margin to Mainstream*. For nineteen years, Rashid worked as a groundskeeper at Wayne State University while teaching courses in creative writing and American studies both there and at Detroit's Marygrove College.

Thug Nun

The bell rings and
Sister Mary Rodrigue
pushes Paul Jedro
to the floor—

Never ignore
this nun who never
teaches
'cause there's no
lesson she'd
learn well enough—

The principal forever
explaining the riddle of
her violence to angry
confused parents willing
to be swayed 'cause they'd
paid for this.

It is late October of 1975.
It is fourth hour freshman
English and
Sister Mary Router
reads "The Highwayman" to a
dazed and jittery room
of Chicanos Arabs Blacks
Irish and Poles—

This is Holy Redeemer High
and a mad woman stalks
the hall like no bad dream—
like no poem you ever
failed to understand.

Forget the hall pass—
She'd hit you for looking
at her the wrong way
For looking at her the
right way—

She broke all
the rules our culturally
sensitive lay folks
and sexually tied up
nuns never could.

I think there was
some problem—some
trigonometric thing
left dangling in her
frontal lobe—

And we were just
in the way so
her discipline
made no sense—
and she prepared us
for the world.

A Loved One Will Do

You know this feeling:
a discussion becomes an argument—
someone yells at you while accusing
you of yelling or
spits words of teeth
that render you vicious—
Someone rips you out of
your world and into
their wound
and you are ruined—
you start yelling hellfire
from your own wounds—
anything to get out of this—
Outside old reason
akin to kin and
aching to pin it on
anyone nearest—
The walls too thin
for all the screaming
and the neighbors happy
not to be you.

Keeping the Knife

The water is too hot to
        wash dishes I
        get too clean
Trying to wash off
        what won't
And after finishing the
        dishes and silverware
I'm left with this single
        paring knife—
Three inch blade wooden
        handle angular
        point—
Knife of the woman I
        just stopped
        living with for
        three years and
        change

I've purged the house of
        her delivering to her new
        space every remainder
        every reminder
But this knife—
        part of a set
        this one small blade
        I kept

My father's people say
        never to give or accept
        knives as gifts—

That it invites a cutting
        of relationships and—
        almost consciously—
        I keep
        to that belief

I wonder then what
        consequence I
        attract by
        keeping this—
        not as a gift
But as a small passive
        theft

She's never asked for it back
She never kept track—
        I did that—
Which is why she left
        so much behind

Anyhow
        What's this knife
        do for me now?
What safety?
What threat?
What now to cut at?

Lady Macbeth

I had an epiphany Sunday while
You were visiting family in the South:
I miss the old silence of Sundays—
my mornings turned to afternoons off the clock,
when I could zone and scribble
and pretend I was a poet.

Since we've married, Sunday's become
a stage for your great and angry
performance: the profoundest house cleaning
I've ever been forced out-of-house
not to witness—
a ritual purge that, even as I
see it and imagine you
ramming my foot with the Hoover,
makes me lonely and wondering
where you are.
Whatever Sundays have become,
I can only breathe on the earth of your air—

And but there it is:
One more double-bind—
The poem that loves you written
only 'cause you've left me
lonely without your dangerous vacuum and
your eyes—
so certain of some filthy thing,
lurking inside us or out,
warranting obliteration.

Sekeena Shaben

Sekeena Shaben was born in Canada and studied at the Jack Kerouac School of Disembodied Poetics. Her poetry and fiction, which have appeared in numerous journals and anthologies in Canada and the United States, were recently set to music in American composer Libby Larsen's *This Unbearable Stillness: Songs from the Balcony*. Shaben, the author of the poetry book *Regular Joe*, lives in New York City, where she is an attorney who works as a public defender.

une demi-vierge

when i was a woman
i thought
stay with the ones who won't
master you that way
the ones who let you remain
hidden; not crossed

i'm not afraid of being conquered
but what is this cavernous emptiness
that surrounds the lining of the flesh
poise; strength frightened mostly by the shell
collapsing
the underneath curling up
and over

i would give my soul away
to finally close the creaking
inanimate door from the distraction
not madness like artaud
that's too poetic for this
this is a far simpler notion of forgetting

on my feet
head out a 5 story new york loft
i sneak a look at the pavement below
love
tap tap tap
on the back of the chair
i hear the clicking of love
someone else's love that repeats itself
rebounds off the grey vapid ceiling of my skull

i climb a ladder
white
wooden
steps
up
to try and snatch this thing
before it reaches the top of me
hands gripping and slipping around the texture
of an unknown leaking
not from the heart
but pouring out of gutted holes in the chest

the same words
the same notes
are on my cd player every day
"in these lines from time to time"
she croons to me
and i wonder who hollowed out her cheeks that way
i will tell you half of what's in my heart
and half i will stuff
back down in my throat
like cotton, soft
in a jar

i hear the
tap tap tap
again
a spoon against a tin cup?
not a knock at the door
and time is not for us anymore
if only i could remain
spaceless
without time
crouched beneath this desk
in this room
which is not mine

i'll let them come for me i think
seems it's better to let them have their way
take me anywhere but here
let them wrap my cool skin
in their words
better than these
i've already buried the rest of me
somewhere else
so this
this part of me
they can have

no response

the red the green the light
the sidewalk beating into open rain
my hand on the glass
echoes
into some time lost memory
a guitar wakens my half open ice blocked mind locked grey
distance flattens and rolls between pavement and yellow lines
between this forward
this movement of your faltering
behind a 3 A.M.
plane touching down hard
and the last peruvian lady of discontent
she said we speak of deep things
i say we speak in the contrary bored ordinary language of lies
no center point
no connection to the martyr drum machine
and my mongolian chess master winner
just my skin in that wet predictable recourse of rain
just your half naked sprawled wandering ass on my canvas
in my room
with my words
with my hand on the wall to brace the inevitable falling
from your forever shifting

the geometry of glass

in a circle
wandering down the length
of an edged glass jar
rounded then flat
the enclosures
a way of stopping
how is it that i have opened you up
this foreign hour?
the splitting of minutes
severing material glass formed
forced; disclosed
designed only for shutting

i sit
waiting
for the shadow of a bottle
within a doorframe
something resembling a container
to be placed before me
not like the other (a brown thin lipped bottle
on a window sill
near a tea cup
near a seared
unmentionable kind of flower)

this one is clear
isolated
imported
portented from faith
resurrected up from a sidewalk

a trashcan revelation
so far away from sunflowers
and indigo prairie landscaped
with white borders

and so finally
in the winsome endsome
i am presented with
a paper cup
placed on a thin steel plate
matted
cloudy
stained shut
lid over the lips
closing everything down
you have, i think
closed everything down
the lashes
the fingers closing
the body bend curling in
tightening around
the impossibility
the now realized improbability
of a transparent glass light
tube shaped
beam ridden (i'd hoped)
to fill in the space
between an empty
doorframe square

Deema K. Shehabi

Deema K. Shehabi was born in Kuwait in 1970, to Palestinian parents. She came to the United States to attend Tufts University, where she studied history and international relations, and also earned a master's degree in journalism from Boston University. Her poems, widely published and translated into Arabic, Farsi, and French, search for "the interconnectedness" that results from "exile spaces of youth and adulthood." She lives in the San Francisco Bay area with her husband and two sons.

Portrait of Summer in Bossey, 15 Years since Her Death

1.

When debris dissolves in the morning breeze,
I arrive to the house of half-breed poplars,
and my child says, *God lives at the far end of lightning—*

but here there are only rock shadows, arching clouds,
and we bend and open to last night's visitor: my mother
on alabaster stairs, saying she has uncovered Gaza

in desiccant cracks of the earth. Her stories are currents
that glide out of her, gliding like my father
as he returns from towing the mountain behind him—

my bedroom window is wide open,
the earth is reeking of shallow sleep,
and he says, *There is no God but One.*

2.

What labors through shallow sleep? What aches in my mother
so that she bows her dark ochre head to the lyrics
of Sabah Fakri: *It's been too long: I miss you as you are the light*

of my eyes, eyes belling with water, as they followed her father
who walked to the podium with flowers strewn at his feet
to unveil Gaza's first statue of liberty. It later crumbled in the square—

first its long plaintive shadow, then the blue hush of the crumble,
but she is not sure what salted the roots of his heart: the death of her
     young sister
or field upon field of exile—he walked for weeks until he reached the border

of Lebanon, the sky rearranging the evidence of place behind him:
So I told her: let no guard stand in our way.
You've lighted my night, you most loved of visitors.

3.

Is this the calamity of roots? Are these the bleeding minutes,
the choked tendrils of love surrounding our life? I tell my father
that when she died, her oldest brother carried a faint smile and said:

angels have brief respite on earth, but my father is too solemn for stories
     tonight.
Tomorrow they will chop down the blue-green spruce she planted—
it obstructs the view of the Geneva fountain from the terrace, the
     fountain that

purred and spun, suddenly attacking passersby, my mother slipping, her
children and friends in slivers behind her. For days, our bellies lunged
     towards laughter,
but my father is inaudible in the rain-lift of a night's storm.

4.

I carry her voice within me like all the living carry the retreating voices of their dead, those white breaths that we seldom hear unless we're afflicted: our arms swollen with water, our breasts bleeding and blistering, the dark-gray shred of our lungs. Then other words sewn into our mouths until the time comes when they are unthreaded. The blunt sobs of her oldest brother bending and opening every doorway of the house. Her body washed in the full light of afternoon. Are these the captured shapes of love?

5.

Were it not for the sudden blue-green gaze of sky, I would have asked my
    father
for a story, and he would have told me he's known love.

6.

In the beginning, my brother and I plowed like Vikings through the village of Bossey, finding the smoky dungeon where the Duke tucked his enemies away from sunlight's unquieting script on the horizon, from the scent of

old, bruised apples hidden beneath paper-soft trees, and from the rows of
crimson rows shrubs that atoned for all the violence it took to make this
    place as
beautiful as legend. We ignored the sky as it crushed water on the blades of

crosses, the blades bending and opening. My brother and I chased
    sparrows that
flew towards the mountain. Later, we fell into the grass, beneath billions
    of moon
shards, our parents sitting on the terrace, their sentences unthreading the
    dark.

7.

The truest story: My grandfather was the mayor of Gaza, a man who walked where anyone would follow. He wrapped warnings around his children: *If disgraced, I will sell my belongings and move to Switzerland.* That my mother would be buried in a Swiss cemetery—wrapped by a mountain that throws the sun back to clouds—he would never know. I bathe her grave—sheet upon sheet of cool water stored in stone basins, all the while my ears pressed against the ambush of words told long ago: *If she doesn't die young, I will cut my tongue out and eat it.*

8.

Along rock shadow, my child and I stare at purple flowers that gallop towards the statue of mother cradling son—the mother's face bending and opening to the grief that hadn't yet materialized at that moment. *We're lost,* I say, and my child is flying towards the sparrows, and they are gliding across the mountain.

Migrant Earth

So, tell me what you think of when the sky is ashen?
—Mahmoud Darwish

I could tell you that listening is made for the ashen sky,
and instead of the muezzin's voice, which lingers like
    weeping at dawn,
I hear my own desire, as I lay my lips against my mother's cheek.

And when I kneel down beside her, I recall her blistering
pleas the day she flung open the gates of her house
    for children fleeing from tanks.

My mother is from Gaza, but what do I know of the migrant earth,
as I enter a Gazan rooftop and perform ablutions in the ashen
    forehead of my skin, my soul journeying and wrinkling with
    homeland?

I could tell you that I parted with my mother at the homeland
    of skin. In the dream,
my lips were bruised, her body was whole again, and we danced
    naked in the street.

There is no child who understands absence past the softness
    of palms.

As though it is praise in my father's palms as he washes
    my mother's body in the final ritual.

As though it is God's pulse that comes across her cheek
    and vanishes.

Matthew Shenoda

A Coptic poet and activist, Matthew Shenoda received an American Book Award for his first book, *Somewhere Else*, which was also named a book of the year by *Poets & Writers Magazine*. "As much about oppression and rebellion as they are about wordplay and jazz," his poems "leap from contemporary urban America to pre-industrial Egypt, trying to make sense of the disparity." A regular contributor to *Voices of the Middle East and North Africa* on KPFA Pacifica Radio, he lives in South Berkeley and is a faculty member of the College of Ethnic Studies at San Francisco State University.

Relics

Scrabbling bones together like a gathering of river stones

Bones become sacred
Human remains, memories of cartilage
Piled centuries high
Skulls and leg remnants begin to tell the stories of before.

I am the once-severed arm of a young girl
Scrambling for a foothold in this desert
Where once my enemy chased did not live

I am the fingers of a woman whose knuckles live beneath a
      flower box

We remember each other through these bones
Through the songs of calcium deficiency and famine strings that
      strum us into night
We are the gathering of old-timers whose eye sockets tell stories
      of victory

We are a memory shaped by vertebrae
Clappers of rhythm disassembled by the skeletons of time

I am the keeper of a man whose only hope was grounding toil
Scrubbing my skin with the earth for food

I am the elbow of children whose eyes twitched at the thought
    of cold

I am the shin of garbage collectors building stamina for a city
    to come

We are a memory shaped by vertebrae
Clappers of rhythm disassembled by the skeletons of time
We are the dissipating cartilage of our great-grandchildren's
    memory holding to their sockets by a sinew of hope

Making sense of these bones we reassemble history
Making ancestral tapestries in the shape of retaining walls

We are a memory shaped by vertebrae
Clappers of rhythm disassembled by the skeletons of time

You are the skin behind the clouds

A Prayer for My People

That one day
we will wish
to be nothing more
than what we are.

That we will see
within ourselves
the liberation of nations, of concrete.

That we will understand
the inevitability
in the lines of our hands.

> There is a war raging in our backyard
> With it my sister's spirit burns

That the fire of my sister's spirit
will consume our enemies
& burn our streets clean.

> There's a system of mangled necks
> Whose heads speak with oracle tongues

That we should learn to walk
with wounded feet

That our eyes must be liberated
from their granite

That our hands re-root themselves
from the pools of acid rain

There's a river forming in the bureaucrat's head
Its water made from rusted milk

That we may understand this false constructed world
& know:

Holy things
Do not die!

In Passing

There is something inside
each of us
that scurries toward the past
in our bodies a rooted history
perhaps in the balls of our feet
a microscopic yearning
that floats inside that sphere
yearning in a language we've forgotten.

History is too in our knees
in the ball that pops
& twists as we journey.

And for those of us blessed to be old
& for those of us blessed to be young
it lives inside the tiny ball of skin
deep inside the belly button
tickles recollections from our tongues
stories of stories from then—

history lives in circles & spheres

floating

always suspended

waiting for release.

Language

Incessant, pushing for the struggle
of re-generation
      one hurricane
replaces another
just when the island has been rejuvenated

Living in kaleidoscope cities
urban twisted metal sculptures
piles of moving fabric
& hair
all that hair, braided together
like a downtown skyline
woven through towers
with a one-two break-beat

Even these buildings have rhythm
metalworker songs
& saw blade scratches
      take them as a symbol
of our rise-up stance
educate our children for a second chance

Ain't no three strikes in the world I live in

We speak forgiveness
like giraffe tongues
long & ready to unravel

We speak change
in the language of the playground
the dialect of freeways and b-ball courts

We understand that nothing happens without a declaration
        even independence

So we declare this place our home
and push forward with those who push
& move past the ones whose feet can catch no rhythm
whose lives remain cemented in a history
unchanged   plagued by the parliament of greed

We declare an eastern expansion
a manifest where the west must rest
& leave its tired self behind

We speak ancestor codes of
handshake body language
& "brother I got your back"

We speak cross-generational tongues
of bilingual *I love you*s
& grand-parental recognition

We break things down to the critical
so that each generation can link to the next
        without severance

We speak in the grand tongue humanity
a language without saliva
an underground dialect
whose code will be deciphered
and whose only script will read:

"Daughter, son, we're ready for you."

From Scetis to Sohag

I

make my face to be like sand
history leaking between brick & mortar
an effervescence of earth
windows of Baramos
shutters of sweeping sky

II

we move across atlantic schism
sail the memory of the forgotten
shed our feet
to touch rock
in this our ancestral home

III

to Him that divided the Red Sea into parts
an inheritance
outstretched in this heat.
Creator, make me a gazelle who
roams these cliffs an eternity

IV

spin the wheat of our sustenance
rejoice in this toil
orbit the planet of palm and date
set free the tongue of want
grind, revolution, grind

V

on the mount of Ansina
I speak green across the valley
Each word a prayer
Psalm-memory deep within this rock
Revelation seekers

VI

by the staff of my elders
I will walk in the line
that they have walked
unlock the gaze from beneath my tomb
& rise like frankincense

VII

and what if we were a cavalcade
into eternity
steer our mules into eternal pastures
take with us nothing more
than color and faith?

VIII

Dayr al-Barsha
painted like marrow & bone
each line a symphonic everlasting
unfurling the wings of the rekhyt
so that we may enter like lotus

IX

falcon became raven
anubis—lion

my elders, open armed in habitation
make yourselves of this place
so as never to remain here

X

etched on the surface of our village
a marker of our existence
dry hooks colored with the past
rising with childhood dreams
beyond any affliction

XI

in this byword world
we rise to the taste of salt
make edible our seeds
and cover the village
with our half-eaten shells

XII

can we read papyrus in neon
understand our course by way of this
foreign illumination
compressed under night sky
by this, the only river's edge?

XIII

peace must come before the name
find the swelling, in the river of your spine
learn to read the eyes of another
this modern hieroglyphics
this modern day tome

XIV

we learn our names by water
blessed in the river of struggle
and from beneath the dome, recount:
mubarak al-ati bism al-Rubb
mubarak al-ati bism al-Rubb

XV

wondrous is your song
dusk-chant
rippling through the palm fronds
awaiting
eastern resurrection

Zaid Shlah

"As much at home with the expansive Qasida tradition as with the work of Ezra Pound, William Carlos Williams, and Derek Walcott," Zaid Shlah's poems blend contemporary voices with the ancient traditions of Iraqi and Arabic poetry. Shlah's first book is *Taqism*. A native of Calgary, Canada, Shlah is the recipient of an American Academy of Poets Award and lectures at the New College of California.

Thirty-Three Beads on a String

1

I woke from the nightmare
of a gutted *maqam*.

2

Not because I have
not yet bled my life

in yellow, but because
minarets sky downwards,
looking for purple births.

3

One burly buffalo
shrouded in hooves
and hot breath.

4

Because the skin
is not yet numb,

and the lights
are not flickering,

I will continue to sip
at my hot tea, and stare
at the dust coloured noon.

5

One white *dishdadha* screams
with the brilliance of red.

6

Can you hear them—
the melodious intent, the
glimmering oud in their eyes?

7

Faith, stitch by seam,
a garment I have sewn
to my skin.

8

Whatever remains of Al-Gubbenchi's
1932 Cairo studio recording, lives
between the old cobble-stoned quarter,
and my still-warm mahogany ear.

9

I should've gotten
up to shake his hand,

this uncomfortable tension
between me and God.

10

Medina, its streets adorned
with smells from the bazaar, yet
I have chosen to adorn myself
in the still concrete of columns.

11

I'm for the transcription
of the Arabic—sweet spread
over toast, a dark syrup from
dates.

12

Last night Al-Gubbenchi
dreamt of his father's fallen
tooth.

13

In the morning he howled
a song in the name of his father;
Iraq's new fathers weep at
the birth of their sons.

14

Do not cry for Leila or for Hind,
but drink the red wine, and grow
your love doubly, one for the ruby
in the cup, the other for its rouge
upon your cheek.

15

Bombs raked the eyes of the
sleeping Assyrian gods.

16

As if it were only a sandbox,
a few worthless grains of sand.

17

I'll cut for you the last swath
of blue from the sky, sever my
hand if you'll let me

but for five minutes more,
leave me to sleep without the
knowledge of war.

18

A quanoun weeps
near the funeral of music.

19

Having been occupied,
notes mourn for the
loss of their song.

20

I'm for a concert of horses;
the origin of gazelles leapt up
from the heart of Al-Gubbenchi.

21

Had you made small steps into
the desert inside us, or listened
for the guttural lodged deep within
our throats, you would have come
bearing gifts.

22

I have nothing in red
that I would not abide
in green.

23

Al-Mutanabbi wrote the
heart of our silken *tarab*;
what need have we for you?

24

No poem is ever enough red—
but that its blood might river
through the life of its people.

25

Beneath the desert-sun,
a cage in Abu Ghraib,
one man by one man by one man,
breathe six.

26

Thousands of tons rung
sonorous from the sky.

27

Black eyed woman,
the street-dogs are running
wild, will you save me?

28

Simple white ignorance:
even the desert has gone into hiding.

29

There is no more meaning
here than the crested moon
holds towards a dying grove
of date trees.

30

I'm for the transcription
of the Arabic—*za'tar zate*
over fire-baked bread.

31

The twin rivers have already
carved for us a history, our poets
have already explained to us
the desert; by what right have
you come?

32

Who of you has seen
the rustic crane in the tree,

no chimes, but for its delicate
wide beak, ushers an intemperate
reprieve.

33

Thirty-three beads on a string,
why pretend to know beyond
the presence   of a click.

David Williams

David Williams is the grandson of Lebanese immigrants whose last name was anglicized from Melhem. Williams is the author of two poetry books, *Traveling Mercies* and *Far Sides of the Only World*, and his poems have appeared in such journals as the *Atlantic Monthly*, the *Kenyon Review*, the *Hayden's Ferry Review*, and *Ploughshares*. His poems demonstrate "an exquisite instinct for capturing one moment that might summarize centuries of struggle" and bear "witness to the most human of all testaments, love." He lives with his family in Worcester, Massachusetts.

Almost One

Airport security recognized my roots. The poor guy at the metal detector trembled and waved in reinforcements. I offered coins, keys, belt buckle, wanted to comfort them all, barely stifled a sudden longing to shout something Whitmanesque. My over-emotional nature inclines me to fanatical fantasies. I want to slip into terminals and depots, anywhere people wait hurriedly, neither here nor there, and seduce them into dancing in lines and circles that eventually join hands in one great spiral. Otherwise I'm afraid someday they might start screaming for blood, if only not to feel so small and alone. Such grandiosity and paranoia, not uncommon among my kind, is cancelled out by an equally characteristic fatalism, which leaves me speechless—a condition hard to spot among minorities, since we can barely get a word in edgewise. So many people can't wait to tell us, with a mathematician's pride, that they've got us figured out. Most generalizations, mine included, are blunt instruments, but some at least have the epic sweep of a memory ferociously repressed, or the momentum of the poor

Legionnaire in that long dying roll down a sand dune in *Beau Geste*. If I try to mention individuals—my cousins, for instance—are huddled defenseless at this very moment under an artillery duel in Beirut, the best of them might smile wanly and say, "It's been going on for two thousand years." But I understand. Who wouldn't pull back, if they could, from the chaos of grief? Exchanges with the dark ones carry risk. Ask the British. Ask the French. Among Arabs their soldiers found victory in places so extreme, they could never get home again, their businessmen cleaned up but lost their children in the desert, their academicians abandoned their meters to stalk malnourished boys, and to this day the sterile places grow. Rational men in the capitals of the practical can always accommodate a tyrant so long as he's only killing wogs. Then one day the anguish in the hollows and ghettos resounds in the finest districts, the flags unfurl, and everyone attributes their hatred to God. "Arabia" and "the West" keep bringing out the worst in each other, and what could save all our lives can barely be heard. And I, neither here nor there, got through the metal detector, with a double legacy and a double grief, the way, you might say, a camel carries water.

Privacy

So what if I outsmarted a fish
I found beautiful and didn't need to eat?
The pickerel's mouth was around the hook—
one more instant he'd bite and be torn.
I jiggled a warning down the line,
and he backed off quick and smooth.

Across the pond a woman came down,
waded in so far and stopped,
but kept throwing out a stick
for her dog to return
while light off the water
dappled up her thighs.

She thought she was alone
so I turned away.

I remember how my father always entered the water
shyly, carefully wetting his skin
like a shepherd smearing an orphaned lamb
with another ewe's blood so she'd claim it.
Once he swam out so far alone, he didn't
know the way back when dark surprised him.
Then someone on shore he never met,
thinking of something else,
flicked on a light and he didn't drown.

Breath

The people I come from were thrown away
as if they were nothing, whatever they might have
said become stone, beyond human patience,
except for the songs. But what is their daily
breath against all the ardent, cunning
justifications for murder?

The stunned drone of grief becomes the fierce,
tender undertone that bears up the world,

steady as a river grinding soil out of stone.
I'm thirsty for words to join that song—
cupped hands at the spring, a cup of
rain passed hand to hand, rain pooled
on stone, a living jewel, a clear
lens trembling with our breath.

In Praise of the Potato

Potato, sojourner north, first sprung
from the flanks of volcanoes, plainspoken kin

to bright chili and deadly nightshade,
sleek eggplant and hairy tobacco,

we could live on you alone if we had to,
and scorched-earth marauders never bothered you much.

I love you because your body's a stem,
your eyes sprout, and you're not in the Bible,

and if we did not eat your strength,
you'd drive it up, into a flower.

Eliot Khalil Wilson

Eliot Khalil Wilson, a native of Virginia, received his Ph.D. in critical theory and American drama from the University of Alabama. His poems, which have garnered awards from the Academy of American Poets and a fellowship from the National Endowment for the Arts, "enliven us . . . make us more suspicious of our work-a-day lives." *The Saint of Letting Small Fish Go*, his first book, won the 2003 Cleveland State Poetry Prize. He teaches creative writing in Minnesota.

Syrian Light and the Leisure of Moths

This must have been how it was
to look down from the orchard hills of Ghota at dawn,
and see Damascus shining far below
and for the last time.

In that light, it must have looked fragile and clean
like acres of card houses.
He had what he could walk with—the *piastres* for his ticket,
flat bread for the slow passage, a folded
name and address.

But this isn't the honeyed light of memory; it's coal dust
from the number three shaft mine in Clearview, West Virginia,
drifting through the windows and doors,
mapping the palms of his small, brown hands,
following him into the house where his wife
is raising nine children and living at the stove
with her ginger root fingers and her cabbage heart
the leaves of which she gives away.

She was a cool round washing machine
wearing a feedsack apron.
He was a lunchpail and a beard full of coal
gone to the mine with the night's last shadow.

Weaving ruined nylons into rugs,
hunting dandelions in spring,
scraping the bones of dinner
into the black dirt of the garden,
they never owned a car, or flew on a plane,
or tasted store-bought eggs.

What was he thinking the night
I found him watching the listless way
the gypsy moths kept flopping their wings against
the screen, a dozen opiated concubines,
each of them yawning and waving a fan?

The Syria that was left for him was in his fig and apricot trees.
Haunting no one in the paid-for house,
settled, but half homeless
until the breath in his black and clouded lungs
refused to move.

Designing a Bird from Memory in Jack's Skin Kitchen

We hated everything below us.
We'd come to hate the ground itself,
to dread the heavy ropes of gravity
drawing us down from blue
to a brooding green
which would billow in tan dust
like waves of fistic clouds.

We'd come to kill
the afternoons, to evade
the blanket heat by flying out of rifle reach
and dropping mortar rounds through the clouds and trees,
our demented resentment entirely non-personal.

I would come to forget Isaac
our Arab gunner with his shell carton filled with baklava
and just how mixed he was
bearded, but awash in after-shave,
dropping incendiary bombs and Hershey bars at the same time,
Viet S'mores we called it.
How he could shoot his .50 caliber,
stoned on hash,
as accurate as fate itself.
How he'd shoot children and dogs,
but not women or birds. *Bad luck*,
he said. *Even when they are dead,*
women and birds remember.

I would forget how we found him later in Song Ngan Valley
because it's not remembering that kills you,
it's forgetting, and I started to forget

how we found him
mixed with the ground and chopper,
repatriated, tangled like a lover,
his broken hand up and open
as if feeling for rain,
or patiently expecting some small gratuity.
The visor of his helmet shining the same
blue-black iridescence
as the glass of Chartres cathedral.

Right here, I tell the tattoo man
giving him my arm,
A blue bird, that certain blue, with black eyes
and rising.

Wedding Vows

. . . and I'd like to add that I will mind like a dog. I will wear whatever you like. I will go wingtip. No more white socks. A necktie stitched to my throat, turtlenecks in August. New York gray or black, only colors that dogs can see. I will know of squash, vermouth, and wedges. I will do all the grilling because I love it so. I will drive the wagon, man the bar, weed-whack compulsively. I will make money, the bed, never a to do.

I will build like an Egyptian, a two-mile pier complex, a five-story deck. I will listen like a bat, attend to the birth of sounds in the back of your throat. I will remember like an Indian elephant, recall requests made of me in a previous life. Your date of birth will be carved in the palm of my hand. I will make good. I will do right. I will sleep on the pegboard on the wall in the garage.

I'll have a tongue like a sperm whale, eyes like a harp seal, biceps like a fiddler crab. I will have gold coins, gold rings, stiff gold hair like shredded wheat. I will be golden at receptions, gold in your pocket, Paganini in your pants. Money will climb over the house like ivy. Excellent credit will be my white whale. I will always. I will everyday. I will nail the seat down. I will let you pretend I am your father.

I will be a priapic automatic teller machine, never down, never a usage fee, a stock prophet, a para-mutual seer, tractable, worshipful no matter what. I will always want to. I won't notice what you don't point out. I will entertain your friends, say how your love saved me. I will convince them. I will talk, really talk, to them. Deep meanings will be toothpicked and passed around.

I will need zero maintenance. I will be a utility or a railroad. There will be no breakdowns or disconnections. I will allow you lovers, Moroccan teenagers and Turkish men. I will adopt them. I will not cry. I will respond to grief by earning more. My sweat will smell like drug money, like white bread baking. I will be as clean as a Mormon, wholesome like Iowa. I will lead. I will be a star, a rock, like Rock Hudson.

Someone Else Happy

The day before my wife said she'd leave,
I took our daughter to the Salvation Army,
where everything comes in that same smell.

She is enchanted by the wonderland of bric-a-brac,
and anything reachable becomes a moment's toy.

It is wonderful for me, too.
The stacks of stained travel luggage from
the Hotel Savoy Majestic and the Dresden Paladium,
the cracked plates, the denuded ornaments,
the single shoes, and torn quilts,
pluck at my instinct to rescue and preserve.

I can't though.
These things are here for a reason,
and in each chipped cup I hear that thought
that considered, then dismissed it.

I never use it.
It will make someone else happy.

After all, I am here to add
my fragments to this space,
purging the house of remnants:
all that's mismatched, the broken frames,
the ruined ties.

I find my daughter flying an F-14
through rows of weary sweaters.
Her left hand holds a naked armless doll up to me.

It's nice, I tell her,
but it can't come home with us.

Ghazal: From Damascus to Donora

Not her eyes, not the remote abstraction of soul, but her fingers.
The music of what happened came through her fingers.

I knew her arms as tulip stems—as young as smooth.
But the ground always knew her ginger root fingers.

And she knew the ground—what it had to give and wouldn't give back.
Knew most seeds as caskets that never grew back to her fingers.

Grafted to a black frozen city where the rivers burn
She'd knead bread—as the dark brimmed blue—with her candle-wax fingers.

Never that shape again—no wood grain or bone delta.
Only clouds, rococo—holding hook and eye—the blue, like her fingers.

FURTHER READING

Unless otherwise noted, all titles listed are poetry publications.

ELMAZ ABINADER

The Children of the Roomje: A Family's Journey from Lebanon (memoir, 1991, 1997)

In the Country of My Dreams (1999)

ETEL ADNAN

The Arab Apocalypse (1989)

Five Senses for One Death (1971)

From A to Z (1982)

The Indian Never Had a Horse (1995)

In/Somnia (2002)

In the Heart of the Heart of Another Country (2005)

Jebu (1973)

Journey to Mount Tamalpais (prose, 1986)

Moonshots (1966)

Of Cities and Women (prose, 1993)

Paris, When It's Naked (prose, 1993)

Sitt Marie Rose (novel, 1990)

The Spring Flowers Own (1990)

There (1997)

KAZIM ALI

The Far Mosque (2005)

The Fortieth Day (2008)

Quinn's Passage (novel, 2004)

ALISE ALOUSI

Wearing Doors Away (1988)

SINAN ANTOON

The Baghdad Blues (2006)

I'jam (novel, 2007)

A Prism: Wet with Wars (2003)

WALID BITAR

2 Guys on Holy Land (1993)

Bastardi Puri (2005)

The Empire's Missing Links (2008)

Maps with Moving Parts (1988)

HAYAN CHARARA

The Alchemist's Diary (2001)

The Sadness of Others (2006)

SHARIF S. ELMUSA

Grape Leaves: A Century of Arab American Poetry (coedited collection, with Gregory Orfalea, 1988, 2000)

MARIAN HADDAD

Saturn Falling Down (2003)

Somewhere between Mexico and a River Called Home (2004)

SUHEIR HAMMAD

Born Palestinian, Born Black (1996)

Drops of This Story (memoir, 1996)

ZaatarDiva (2005)

SAM HAMOD

After the Funeral of Assam Hamady (1971)

The Arab Poems, the Muslim Poems (2000)

Dying with the Wrong Name: New & Selected Poems 1968–1980 (1980)

The Famous Blue Mounds Scrapbook (1972)

The Famous Boating Party (1970)

The Famous Boating Party II (1973)

The Holding Action (1969)

Just Love Poems for You (2006)

Surviving in America (with Anselm Hollo and Jack Marshall, 1971)

NATHALIE HANDAL

Language for a New Century: Contemporary Poetry from the Middle East, Asia, and Beyond (coedited collection, with Tina Chang and Ravi Shankar, 2008)

The Lives of Rain (2005)

The Neverfield (1999)

The Poetry of Arab Women (edited collection, 2001)

SAM HAZO

An American Made in Paris (1978)

As They Sail (1999)

Blood Rights (1968)

The Color of Reluctance (1986)

Discovery and Other Poems (1958)

A Flight to Elsewhere (2005)

The Holy Surprise of Right Now (1996)

Just Once (2002)

Listen with the Eye (1964)

My Sons in God (1965)

Nightwords (1987)

Once for the Last Bandit (1972)

The Past Won't Stay Behind You (1993)

Picks: 1966–1991 (1991)

Quartered (1974)

The Quiet Wars (1962)

Silence Spoken Here (1988)

Thank a Bored Angel (1983)

To Paris (1981)

Twelve Poems (1972)

LAWRENCE JOSEPH

Before Our Eyes (1993)

Codes, Precepts, Biases, and Taboos: Poems 1973–1993 (2005)

Curriculum Vitae (1988)

Into It (2005)

Lawyerland (prose, 1997)

Shouting at No One (1983)

FADY JOUDAH

The Earth in the Attic (2008)

MOHJA KAHF

E-Mails from Scheherazad (2003)

The Girl in the Tangerine Scarf (novel, 2006)

Western Representations of the Muslim Woman from Termagant to Odalisque (criticism, 1999)

PAULINE KALDAS

Dinarzad's Children: An Anthology of Contemporary Arab American Fiction (coedited collection, with Khaled Mattawa, 2004)

Egyptian Compass (2006)

Letters from Cairo (2007)

LISA SUHAIR MAJAJ

Etel Adnan: Critical Essays on the Arab-American Writer and Artist (coedited collection, with Amal Amireh, 2002)

Going Global: The Transnational Reception of Third World Women Writers (coedited collection, with Amal Amireh, 2000)

Intersections: Gender, Nation and Community in Arab Women's Novels (edited collection, 2002)

These Words (2003)

What She Said (2005)

JACK MARSHALL

Arabian Nights (1987)

Arriving on the Playing Fields of Paradise (1984)

Bearings (1970)

Bits of Thirst (1976)

Chaos Comics (1994)

The Darkest Continent (1967)

Floats (1972)

From Baghdad to Brooklyn: Growing Up in a Jewish-Arabic Family in Mid-Century America (memoir, 2005)

Gorgeous Chaos (2002)

The Steel Veil (2008)

Millennium Fever (1996)

Sesame (1993)

Surviving in America (with Anselm Hollo and Sam Hamod, 1971)

KHALED MATTAWA

Dinarzad's Children: An Anthology of Contemporary Arab American Fiction (coedited collection, with Pauline Kaldas, 2004)

Ismailia Eclipse (1995)

Post-Gibran: Anthology of New Arab American Writing (coedited collection, with Munir Akash, 2000)

Zodiac of Echoes (2003)

D. H. MELHEM

A Different Path: An Anthology of RAWI (coedited collection, with Leila Diab, 2000)

Blight (novel, 1995)

The Cave (novel, 2007)

Children of the House Afire/More Notes on 94th Street (1976, 2005)

Conversation with a Stonemason (2003)

Country: An Organic Poem (1998)

Gwendolyn Brooks: Poetry and the Heroic Voice (criticism, 1987)

Heroism in the New Black Poetry (criticism, 1990)

New York Poems (2005)

Notes on 94th Street (1972, 1979, 2005)

Poems for You (2000)

Rest in Love (1975, 1978, 1995)

Stigma (novel, 2007)

PHILIP METRES

Behind the Lines: War Resistance Poetry on the American Home Front since 1941 (criticism, 2007)

Catalogue of Comedic Novelties: Selected Poems of Lev Rubinstein (translation, 2004)

Instants (2006)

A Kindred Orphanhood: Selected Poems of Sergey Gandlevsky (translation, 2003)

Primer for Non-Native Speakers (2004)

To See the Earth (2008)

HAAS M. MROUE

Beirut Seizures (1993)

ADELE NE JAME

Field Work (1996)

Inheritance (1989)

NAOMI SHIHAB NYE

19 Varieties of Gazelle (2005)

Different Ways to Pray (1980)

Fuel (1998)

Hugging the Jukebox (1982)

I Feel a Little Jumpy (coedited collection, with Paul B. Janeczko, 1999)

Mint (1991)

Red Suitcase (1994)

The Space between Our Footsteps (edited collection, 1998)

This Same Sky (edited collection, 1996)

What Have You Lost? (edited collection, 2001)

The Words under the Words (1995)

Yellow Glove (1986)

You & Yours (2005)

GREGORY ORFALEA

The Arab Americans: A History (prose, 2006)

The Capital of Solitude (1988)

Grape Leaves: A Century of Arab American Poetry (coedited collection, with Sharif S. Elmusa, 1988, 2000)

Messengers of the Lost Battalion (prose, 1997)

Pictures at an Exhibition (1977)

Up All Night: Practical Wisdom from Mothers and Fathers (coedited collection, with Barbara Rosewicz, 2004)

SEKEENA SHABEN

Regular Joe (1995)

MATTHEW SHENODA

Seasons of Lotus, Seasons of Bone (2009)

Somewhere Else (2005)

ZAID SHLAH

Taqsim (2006)

DAVID WILLIAMS

Far Sides of the World (2004)

Traveling Mercies (1993)

ELIOT KHALIL WILSON

The Saint of Letting Small Fish Go (2003)

ACKNOWLEDGMENTS

ELMAZ ABINADER: "Living with Opposition," "What We Leave Behind," "The Birds." Copyright © 1999 by Elmaz Abindaer. Originally appeared in *In the Country of My Dreams* (Sufiwarrior Publications). Reprinted by permission of the author. "This House, My Bones." Copyright © by Elmaz Abinader. Reprinted by permission of the author.

ETEL ADNAN: "Transcendence." Copyright © by Etel Adnan. Reprinted by permission of the author. "The Arab Apocalypse." Copyright © 1989 by Etel Adnan. Reprinted by permission of the author.

SALADIN AHMED: "Ibn Sina." Copyright © by Saladin Ahmed. Originally appeared in *Margie: The American Journal of Poetry.* Reprinted by permission of the author. "Ghazal," "Over the Phone, One of Our Hero's Close Personal Homeboys Recounts Life in a College Town," "The Third World Werewolf Speaks to Our Hero of Life in the Financial Zone." Copyright © by Saladin Ahmed. Reprinted by permission of the author.

KAZIM ALI: "The Black Madonna at Chartres." Copyright © by Kazim Ali. Originally appeared in *Sentence: A Journal of Prose Poetics.* Reprinted by permission of the author. "Gallery," "The Year of Summer," and "Journey" from *The Far Mosque.* Copyright © 2005 by Kazim Ali. Reprinted with the permission of Alice James Books.

ASSEF AL-JUNDI: "Flying." Copyright © 1993 by Assef Al-Jundi. Originally appeared in *Poets of the Lake 2, Our Own Clues.* Reprinted by permission of the author. "Nostalgic," "Apprentice." Copyright © by Assef Al-Jundi. Reprinted by permission of the author.

ALISE ALOUSI: "Lipstick Series," "Mayfly," What to Count," "Lynndie's Other Voice." Copyright © Alise Alousi. Reprinted by permission of the author.

NUAR ALSADIR: "Bats," "The Garden." Copyright © 2000 by Nuar Alsadir. Originally appeared in the *Kenyon Review.* Reprinted by permission of the author. "The Riddle of the Shrink." Copyright © 2005 by Nuar Alsadir. Originally appeared in *Slate Magazine*. Reprinted by permission of the author.

SINAN ANTOON: "Wrinkles: on the wind's forehead," "A Photograph," "A Letter," "Delving," "Sifting." Copyright © by Sinan Antoon. Reprinted by permission of Harbor Mountain Press.

WALID BITAR: "Looking You in the Back of the Head," from *2 Guys on Holy Land*. Copyright © by Walid Bitar. Reprinted by permission of Wesleyan University Press. "Survival of the Fittest," "Progress Report," "A Disposition of the Antiquities," from *Basturdi Puri*. Copyright © by Walid Bitar. Reprinted by permission of The Porcupine's Quill. "Under the Table," from *The Empire's Missing Link,* copyright © by Walid A. Bitar, are used by permission of Signal Editions/Véhicule Press.

AHIMSA TIMOTEO BODHRÁN: "Manos .17." Copyright © by Ahimsa Timoteo Bodhrán. Originally appeared in *Borderlands: Texas Poetry Review*. Reprinted by permission of the author. "Mint." Copyright © by Ahimsa Timoteo Bodhrán. Originally appeared in *Mizna*. Reprinted by permission of the author.

HAYAN CHARARA: "Thinking American." Reprinted from *The Alchemist's Diary.* Copyright © 2001 by Hayan Charara, by permission of Hanging Loose Press. "Washing My Father." Copyright © 2006 by Hayan Charara. Reprinted from *The Sadness of Others,* by permission of Carnegie Mellon University Press. "Usage." Copyright © by Hayan Charara. Originally appeared in *Literary Imagination*. Reprinted by permission of the author.

SHARIF S. ELUMSA: "Flawed Landscape." Copyright © by Sharif S. Elmusa. Originally appeared in *Post-Gibran: Anthology of New Arab American Poetry,* ed. Munir Akash and Khaled Mattawa (Syracuse University Press). Reprinted by permission of the author. "With New Englanders," "Roots." Originally appeared in *Banipal.* Copyright © by Sharif S. Elmusa. Reprinted by permission of the author. "Should You Wish to Stay," "Sun Lines." Copyright © by Sharif S. Elmusa. Reprinted by permission of the author.

HEDY HABRA: "Even the Sun Has Its Dark Side." Copyright © by Hedy Habra. Reprinted by permission of the author. "Milkweed." Copyright ©

1997 by Hedy Habra. Originally appeared in *Sulfur River Review*. Reprinted by permission of the author. "Tea at *Chez Paul's*." Copyright © 2003 by Hedy Habra. Originally appeared in *Nimrod International Journal*. Reprinted by permission of the author.

MARIAN HADDAD: "She Is Not the House of This Black Wing," "Malfunctioning FLOWTRON," "Resurrection." Copyright © by Marian Haddad. Reprinted by permission of Pecan Grove Press and the author. "I have no history here." Copyright © by Marian Haddad. Reprinted by permission of the author.

SUHEIR HAMMAD: "Silence," "exotic," "First Writing Since," "mike check." Copyright © by Suheir Hammad. Reprinted by permission of the author.

SAM HAMOD: "Dying with the Wrong Name." Copyright © by Sam Hamod. Reprinted by permission of the author.

LARA HAMZA: "Advice for Marriage," "My Mother Wore Miniskirts," "Behind Locked Doors, Part I," "Growing Up," "On Eating." Copyright © by Lara Hamza. Reprinted by permission of the author.

NATHALIE HANDAL: "The Warrior," "The Combatant and I," "The Blue Jacket," excerpts from *The Neverfield*. Copyright © by Nathalie Handal. Reprinted by permission of the author.

SAM HAZO: "Intifada," "September 11, 2001," "Just Words," "After Arlington," "The First Sam Hazo at the Last," "The Mutineer," "For Which It Stands." Reprinted from *Just Once: New and Previous Poems*, copyright © 2002, and *A Flight to Elsewhere*, copyright © 2005, by permission of the author and Autumn House Press.

LAWRENCE JOSEPH: "It's Me Shouting at No One," "Do What You Can," "Curriculum Vitae," "Sand Nigger," "I Pay the Price," and "Before Our Eyes," from *Codes, Precepts, Biases, and Taboos: Poems 1973–1993*, by Lawrence Joseph. Copyright © 2005 by Lawrence Joseph. Reprinted by permission of Farrar, Straus and Giroux. "Rubaiyat," "Inclined to Speak," from *Into It*, by Lawrence Joseph. Copyright © 2005 by Lawrence Joseph. Reprinted by permission of Farrar, Straus and Giroux.

FADY JOUDAH: "Morning Ritual," "At a Café," "Sleeping Trees," "Additional Notes on Tea," from *The Earth in the Attic.* Copyright © by Fady Joudah. Reprinted by permission of Yale University Press.

MOHJA KAHF: "My Grandmother Washes Her Feet in the Sink of the Bathroom at Sears," "*Hijab* Scene #1," "*Hijab* Scene #3." Copyright © by Mohja Kahf. Reprinted by permission of the University Press of Florida. "Postcards from Hajar, a Correspondence in Four Parts." Copyright © by Mohja Kahf. Originally appeared in *The Muslim World* (Hartford Seminary, Hartford, Connecticut). Reprinted by permission of the author.

PAULINE KALDAS: "Bird Lessons," "Fraudulent Acts," "My Aunt's Kitchen," "What America Has to Offer," from *Egyptian Compass,* by Pauline Kaldas, © 2006 by Custom Words, Cincinnati, Ohio.

LISA SUHAIR MAJAJ: "In Season." Copyright © by Lisa Suhair Majaj. Originally appeared in *Mizna.* Reprinted by permission of the author. "It Wasn't Poetry." Copyright © by Lisa Suhair Majaj. Originally appeared online on WinningWriters.com. Reprinted by permission of the author. "Arguments." Copyright © by Lisa Suhair Majaj. Originally appeared in *The Poetry of Arab Women: A Contemporary Anthology,* ed. Nathalie Handal (Interlink). An earlier version appeared in *Al Jadid* under the title "Arguments against the Bombing." Reprinted by permission of the author. "I Remember My Father's Hands." Copyright © by Lisa Suhair Majaj. Originally appeared in *The Spirit* and then in *The Space between Our Footsteps,* ed. Naomi Shihab Nye (Simon and Schuster). Reprinted by permission of the author.

JACK MARSHALL: "Walking Across Brooklyn Bridge," "Appalachia Suite," "Crane," "G–D," "The Home-Front," "Place in the Real," from *Gorgeous Chaos: Selected and New Poems 1965–2001.* Copyright © 2002 by Jack Marshall. Reprinted with the permission of Coffee House Press, www.coffeehousepress.org.

KHALED MATTAWA: "Growing Up with a Sears Catalog in Benghazi, Libya," "Watermelon Tales," "The Bus Driver Poem," from *Ismailia Eclipse* (The Sheep Meadow Press, 1995). Copyright © by Khaled Mattawa.

Reprinted by permission of the author. "The Road to Biloxi," "Echo &
Elixir 1," "Echo & Elixir 3," from *Zodiac of Echoes* (Ausable Press, 2003).
Copyright © by Khaled Mattawa. Reprinted by permission of the author.

D. H. MELHEM: *"New York Times,* August 15, 1976, 'As Lebanon Dies,'"
"Broadway Music," "On the tendency toward solipsism in literature."
Children of the House Afire (1976); reprinted in *New York Poems.* Copyright
© 2005 by D. H. Melhem. Syracuse University Press, New York, 2005.
Selections from *Rest in Love* (1975; 2nd ed., 1978); reprinted in *Rest in Love.*
Copyright © 1995 by D. H. Melhem. Confrontation Magazine Press,
Brookville, NY, 1995. Selections from *Country: An Organic Poem.* Copyright
© 1998 by D. H. Melhem. Cross-Cultural Communications, Merrick, NY,
1998. "September 11, World Trade Center, Aftermath," from the sequence
"Requiescant 9/11." Copyright © 2003 by D. H. Melhem. First published
in *Conversation with a Stonemason.* IKON, New York, 2003. Reprinted in
New York Poems. Copyright © 2005 by D. H. Melhem. Syracuse University
Press, New York, 2005.

PHILIP METRES: "One more story he said In a restaurant in Amsterdam,"
"A House Without." Copyright © by Philip Metres. Reprinted by permis-
sion of the author. "Ashberries: Letters." Copyright © by Philip Metres.
Originally appeared in the *New England Review* and then in *Best American
Poetry 2002,* ed. Robert Creeley (Simon and Schuster). Reprinted by per-
mission of the author.

HAAS H. MROUE: "Beirut Survivors Anonymous," "Arabes Despatriados,"
"Civil War." Copyright © by Haas H. Mroue. Reprinted by permission of
the author.

ADELE NE JAME: "Fieldwork, Devil's Lake, Wisconsin," "Anabelle's," "A
Blessing," "A Love Story." Copyright © by Adele Ne Jame. Reprinted by
permission of the author.

NAOMI SHIHAB NYE: "Different Ways to Pray," "The Art of
Disappearing," "Famous," "Breaking My Favorite Bowl," "Blood," "The
Small Vases from Hebron," "What Brings Us Out," "Jerusalem." Copyright
© 2007 by Naomi Shihab Nye. Reprinted by permission of the author.

GREGORY ORFALEA: "War," "The Bomb That Fell on Abdu's Farm," "The Spider," "On the One in the Crook of My Chest." Copyright © by Gregory Orfalea. Reprinted by permission of the author.

KEVIN GERARD RASHID: "Thug Nun," "A Loved One Will Do," "Keeping the Knife," "Lady Macbeth." Copyright © by Kevin Gerard Rashid. Reprinted by permission of the author.

SEKEENA SHABEN: "une demi-vierge," "no response," "the geometry of glass." Copyright © by Sekeena Shaben. Reprinted by permission of the author.

DEEMA K. SHEHABI: "Portrait of Summer in Bossey, 15 Years since Her Death." Copyright © 2006 by Deema K. Shehabi. Originally appeared in *Drunken Boat*. Reprinted by permission of the author. "Migrant Earth." Copyright © 2004 by Deema K. Shehabi. Originally appeared in the *Crab Orchard Review*. Reprinted by permission of the author.

MATTHEW SHENODA: "Relics," "A Prayer for My People," "In Passing," "Language." Copyright © 2006 by Matthew Shenoda. Reprinted from *Somewhere Else* with the permission of Coffee House Press, www.coffee housepress.org. "From Scetis to Sohag." Copyright © by Matthew Shenoda. Reprinted by permission of the author.

ZAID SHLAH: "Thirty-three Beads on a String." Copyright © 2006 by Zaid Shlah. Reprinted from *Taqsim* by permission of the author and Frontenac House.

DAVID WILLIAMS: "Almost One," "Privacy," "Breath," "In Praise of the Potato," from *Traveling Mercies*. Copyright © 1993 by David Williams. Reprinted with the permission of Alice James Books.

ELIOT KHALIL WILSON: "Syrian Light and the Leisure of Moths," "Designing a Bird from Memory in Jack's Skin Kitchen," "Wedding Vows," "Someone Else Happy," "Ghazal: From Damascus to Donora." from *The Saint of Letting Small Fish Go*, by Eliot Khalil Wilson. Copyright © by Eliot Khalil Wilson. Reprinted by permission of the Cleveland State University Poetry Center.

INDEX OF AUTHORS AND TITLES

HAYAN CHARARA was a visiting professor of poetry writing at the University of Texas at Austin in 2005. Before that he taught in New York City. He is the author of two collections of poetry, *The Sadness of Others* (Carnegie Mellon, 2006) and *The Alchemist's Diary* (Hanging Loose, 2001). Born in Detroit, Michigan, to immigrant parents, he currently lives in Texas. He is also a woodworker.